THE U

Wedding Guide

EXPERT TIPS AND SECRETS FOR YOUR DREAM WEDDING

HANNA OLIVAS
ALONG WITH 9 INSPIRING AUTHORS

© 2025 ALL RIGHTS RESERVED.

Published by She Rises Studios Publishing **www.SheRisesStudios.com**.

No part of this book may be reproduced or transmitted in any form whatsoever, electronic, or mechanical, including photocopying, recording, or by any informational storage or retrieval system without the expressed written, dated and signed permission from the publisher and co-authors.

LIMITS OF LIABILITY/DISCLAIMER OF WARRANTY:

The co-authors and publisher of this book have used their best efforts in preparing this material. While every attempt has been made to verify the information provided in this book, neither the co-authors nor the publisher assumes any responsibility for any errors, omissions, or inaccuracies.

The co-authors and publisher make no representation or warranties with respect to the accuracy, applicability, or completeness of the contents of this book. They disclaim any warranties (expressed or implied), merchantability, or for any purpose. The co-authors and publisher shall in no event be held liable for any loss or other damages, including but not limited to special, incidental, consequential, or other damages.

ISBN: 978-1-964619-96-5

TABLE OF CONTENTS

INTRODUCTION 5

The Ultimate Wedding Guide: Saying "Yes" and "I Do"
    By Hanna Olivas 8

Creating Unforgettable Ceremonies: The Journey to "I Do"
    By Denise O'Malley 16

Mindful Radiance: A Bride's Guide to the Breath/Beauty Connection
    By Kenya Elizabeth Aissa, MS 25

From the First Look to the Last Dance: Why Bridal Hair and Makeup Matter
    By Ashley McCombs 37

Unveiling the Perfect Gown: Smart Strategies for Stress-Free Dress Shopping
    By Candice Damele 50

Wedding Planning Marries Wellness
    By Kristin Sullivan 60

Do the *Dang Thing* That Makes You Happy
    By Heather Arra 66

Hire A High Energy Hype Queen: The Wedding Planning Process Explained
    By Callie Rackley Carr 72

Why Experience Matters: The Essential Role of Professional Vendors in Your Wedding
    By Jean Neuhart 84

How to Choose the Right Wedding Officiant for Your Ceremony
    By Beverly Little 99

INTRODUCTION

Planning your wedding should be a joyous and exhilarating experience, a time when you're filled with excitement as you prepare to celebrate the most important day of your life. Yet, it can often feel overwhelming with the myriad of decisions, details, and demands. ***The Ultimate Wedding Guide: Expert Tips and Secrets for Your Dream Wedding*** is here to turn that stress into ease and make your wedding planning process as smooth and delightful as it should be.

This comprehensive guidebook is your trusted companion on your wedding journey, packed with expert advice and insider secrets from the best professionals in the industry. From seasoned wedding planners and photographers to florists, caterers, and more, each chapter is brimming with invaluable knowledge to help you navigate the often-complicated wedding landscape. Whether you're dreaming of finding the perfect dress, securing an enchanting venue, or creating unforgettable moments with unique entertainment, our experts provide the guidance you need to make confident and informed decisions.

Within these pages, you'll also find practical strategies for managing your budget, crafting a seamless timeline, and personalizing every aspect of your celebration to reflect your love story in the most meaningful way. Explore creative DIY ideas, learn how to select the right vendors, and uncover common mistakes to avoid—all with the help of our top-tier professionals.

The Ultimate Wedding Guide is not just a manual; it's a celebration of the magic and challenges that come with planning a wedding. With real-life anecdotes, success stories, and inspiration from couples who've been through it all, this book ensures that you feel empowered and excited about the journey ahead.

Armed with the wisdom and expertise of wedding industry leaders, you'll enter your wedding planning experience feeling confident, prepared, and ready to create the wedding of your dreams.

Hanna Olivas

Founder and CEO of SHE RISES STUDIOS

https://www.linkedin.com/company/she-rises-studios/
https://www.facebook.com/sherisesstudios
https://www.instagram.com/sherisesstudios_llc/
www.SheRisesStudios.com

Author, Speaker, and Founder. Hanna was born and raised in Las Vegas, Nevada, and has paved her way to becoming one of the most influential women of 2022. Hanna is the co-founder of She Rises Studios and the founder of the Brave & Beautiful Blood Cancer Foundation. Her journey started in 2017 when she was first diagnosed with Multiple Myeloma, an incurable blood cancer. Now more than ever, her focus is to empower other women to become leaders because The Future is Female. She is currently traveling and speaking publicly to women to educate them on entrepreneurship, leadership, and owning the female power within.

The Ultimate Wedding Guide: Saying "Yes" and "I Do"

By Hanna Olivas

Weddings are often portrayed as grand celebrations, filled with love, laughter, and unforgettable moments. As you embark on this beautiful journey toward marriage, the words "yes" and "I do" carry profound significance, not just for the ceremony but for the life you will build together. Planning the ultimate wedding is an exciting adventure that requires careful thought and consideration, but it is essential to remember that the true essence of this day lies in the commitment you are making to one another.

In this chapter, we will explore what it means to say "yes" and "I do," what men and women often look for when planning their dream wedding, and the vital tips and insights that can help create a memorable celebration. But more importantly, we will delve into the value of preparing for the marriage itself—an enduring partnership that extends far beyond the wedding day.

The Significance of Saying "Yes" and "I Do"

The moment you say "yes" to your partner is the beginning of a beautiful journey. This affirmative response signifies a commitment to love, support, and cherish one another through life's challenges and triumphs. Saying "yes" is a declaration of trust and partnership, a promise that you will be there for each other, no matter what.

When you stand before family and friends and say "I do," you are making a sacred vow. This moment is a culmination of your love story—a testament to the journey that brought you together and the future you will share. Saying "I do" is not merely about the ceremony; it is an acknowledgment of the profound bond that you are choosing to honor for the rest of your lives.

Understanding Each Other's Dreams and Expectations

Before diving into the logistics of planning your wedding, it is crucial to have open and honest conversations with your partner about your dreams and expectations for the day. Here are some key points to discuss:

Your Vision for the Day: Each partner may have different ideas about what their ideal wedding looks like. Discuss elements such as the venue, style, theme, and atmosphere you both envision. Are you dreaming of an intimate gathering with close family and friends or a grand celebration with hundreds of guests? Understanding each other's visions will help set a foundation for your planning process.

Budget and Priorities: Finances play a significant role in wedding planning. Discuss your budget openly and set realistic expectations. Identify which aspects of the wedding are most important to each of you—whether it's the venue, catering, photography, or entertainment. Knowing where you are willing to invest can help guide your decision-making.

Family and Cultural Considerations: If either of you comes from a family or cultural background that has specific wedding traditions, discuss how you want to incorporate those into your ceremony. Honoring your heritage can add a meaningful layer to your wedding.

Your Relationship Goals: Consider discussing what marriage means to each of you. What are your expectations for the relationship post-wedding? What kind of life do you envision building together? This conversation can help align your goals and foster deeper understanding.

Planning the Ultimate Wedding

Now that you have a clear vision and understanding of each other's expectations, it's time to delve into the logistics of planning your ultimate wedding. Here are some essential tips to help you create a memorable celebration:

1. Choose the Right Venue

The venue sets the tone for your wedding day. When selecting a location, consider the following:

Style: Does the venue reflect your personalities? Whether it's a rustic barn, a lavish ballroom, or a beachside paradise, choose a place that resonates with both of you.

Capacity: Make sure the venue can comfortably accommodate your guest list. Think about whether you want a small, intimate gathering or a larger celebration.

Logistics: Consider the venue's accessibility for your guests. Is it easy to find? Is parking available? Ensure that your guests will feel welcomed and comfortable.

2. Create a Detailed Timeline

A well-organized timeline can help ensure that everything runs smoothly on your wedding day. Here are some key elements to include:

Pre-Wedding Events: Plan out events leading up to the wedding, such as rehearsal dinners and bridal showers.

Ceremony Schedule: Outline the timing of the ceremony, including music, readings, and any special rituals.

Reception Details: Create a timeline for the reception, including speeches, dances, and cake cutting.

3. Personalize Your Ceremony

The ceremony is the heart of your wedding day. Make it personal and meaningful by incorporating elements that reflect your relationship. Here are some ideas:

Vows: Write your own vows to express your love and commitment in a way that is unique to you both.

Readings: Choose readings that resonate with your relationship. These can be excerpts from literature, poetry, or scripture that hold special significance for you.

Rituals: Consider incorporating rituals that symbolize your love and commitment, such as a unity candle lighting, sand ceremony, or handfasting.

4. Curate an Unforgettable Experience for Your Guests

Your wedding day is a celebration of love, and your guests are an integral part of that celebration. Here are ways to make their experience memorable:

Welcome Gifts: Consider providing welcome bags with snacks, beverages, and local information for out-of-town guests.

Interactive Elements: Incorporate interactive elements, such as photo booths, games, or a live band that encourages dancing.

Thank You Notes: Show appreciation for your guests by sending heartfelt thank you notes after the wedding, expressing your gratitude for their presence and support.

5. Plan for the Unexpected

No matter how well you plan, unexpected challenges may arise on your wedding day. Here are tips to handle any surprises gracefully:

Have a Backup Plan: If you're planning an outdoor wedding, consider having an indoor backup in case of inclement weather.

Hire a Day-Of Coordinator: If your budget allows, hire a wedding coordinator to manage the day's logistics, allowing you to focus on enjoying the moment.

Stay Calm and Flexible: Remember that things may not go exactly as planned. Maintain a positive attitude and be willing to adapt if necessary.

Preparing for Marriage: Beyond the Wedding Day

While planning the ultimate wedding is essential, it is equally important to focus on what comes after the celebration: your marriage. Here are some key insights to help you prepare for this lifelong commitment:

1. Communicate Openly and Honestly

Effective communication is the cornerstone of a successful marriage. Make it a habit to engage in open and honest conversations with your partner about your feelings, desires, and concerns. Regular check-ins can help you both stay connected and address any issues before they escalate.

2. Cultivate a Strong Partnership

Marriage is a partnership that requires effort from both sides. Here are ways to strengthen your bond:

Set Goals Together: Discuss your aspirations as a couple, whether they relate to career, family, travel, or personal growth. Setting shared goals can help you work toward a common future.

Support Each Other: Encourage each other's dreams and ambitions. Celebrate successes together and be there for one another during challenging times.

Create Traditions: Establish traditions that are meaningful to you both. Whether it's a monthly date night or an annual vacation, creating shared experiences can strengthen your bond.

3. Navigate Conflict with Grace

Disagreements are a natural part of any relationship. Learning how to navigate conflict with grace and understanding is crucial for a healthy marriage. Here are some strategies:

Practice Active Listening: Make an effort to listen to your partner's perspective without interrupting. Acknowledge their feelings and validate their concerns.

Use "I" Statements: When discussing issues, use "I" statements to express your feelings. For example, say "I feel hurt when..." instead of "You always...". This approach can help prevent defensiveness.

Take Breaks When Needed: If a conversation becomes heated, take a break to cool off before revisiting the discussion. This can help you both approach the situation with a clearer mindset.

4. Prioritize Quality Time Together

In the hustle and bustle of daily life, it's easy to lose sight of each other. Make it a priority to spend quality time together, nurturing your relationship. Here are some ideas:

Plan Regular Date Nights: Schedule time each week or month for date nights. Try new activities or revisit old favorites to keep the spark alive.

Engage in Shared Hobbies: Discover hobbies you can enjoy together, whether it's cooking, hiking, or painting. Engaging in activities you both love can strengthen your connection.

Unplug and Be Present: Create tech-free zones or times where you can focus solely on each other. Put away devices and engage in meaningful conversations.

Conclusion: Embracing the Journey Ahead

As you embark on this journey toward marriage, remember that the ultimate wedding is not just about the day itself but the life you will build together. Saying "yes" and "I do" marks the beginning of a beautiful partnership filled with love, joy, and growth.

Planning the ultimate wedding is an exciting adventure, and the tips shared in this guide can help create an unforgettable celebration. But as you navigate the planning process, do not lose sight of the importance of preparing for the marriage that follows. A successful marriage requires communication, understanding, and a commitment to nurturing your relationship.

Embrace the journey ahead, knowing that each moment—both big and small—will contribute to the beautiful tapestry of your love story. With love, patience, and prayer, you can create not only an amazing wedding day but also a fulfilling and lasting marriage.

Denise O'Malley

CEO of Elevate Wedding Officiant, LLC

https://www.facebook.com/ElevateWeddingOfficiant
https://www.instagram.com/elevateweddingofficiant/
https://elevateweddingofficiant.com/

Denise O'Malley, co-owner of Elevate Wedding Officiant, LLC, and an officiant herself, leads a team of professional public speakers dedicated to crafting unique, unforgettable ceremonies that reflect each couple's personality. Denise joined Elevate as an officiant in 2022, and a year later, she and her husband Bill took over the business to continue its legacy. An accomplished public speaker since childhood, Denise thrives on creating inspiring, memorable moments for every wedding. At Elevate, we honor what couples truly want and thoughtfully incorporate traditional elements when desired. Denise believes in allowing each couple's story to shine, just as she plans to renew her own vows at the venue where she was married—now featuring their old fireplace in the women's restroom. Since 2020, Elevate has received hundreds of 5-star reviews and industry awards for excellence. Denise doesn't just blindly follow traditions—she elevates them.

Creating Unforgettable Ceremonies: The Journey to "I Do"

By Denise O'Malley

Every love story deserves a celebration, and that's what a wedding ceremony is all about. It's a moment where two individuals come together, not just to exchange vows, but to honor their unique relationship and the values that have shaped their journey. A thoughtfully crafted ceremony reflects the couple's love story, capturing the essence of their connection while looking forward to a future filled with shared dreams. This is a time to weave together personal stories, cherished traditions, and heartfelt promises, creating a memorable experience that resonates deeply with everyone present. Ultimately, it's about creating a space where love is celebrated, and the couple's commitment shines brightly.

When couples meet with me for their first consultation, there's a beautiful energy in the air, a palpable excitement as they describe the vision for their wedding. Often, they eagerly share details about their theme, colors, and venue—all the carefully curated touches for the party. Then I ask, *"So, what do you envision for the ceremony itself?"*

That's when I usually see the "deer in the headlights" look. There's a pause, a few laughs, and often an honest, *"That's why we're here with you!"* It's no surprise; for most couples, this is the first time they're planning a wedding, and the ceremony isn't something they've thought about beyond the "I do's." They know they want it to be special, but they're not quite sure how. And that's where my role begins.

After a long career as a corporate executive and business owner, I went looking for a side gig, something that would be different than what I had been doing, use the skills I've accumulated, and be fulfilling. A friend suggested wedding officiating, believing my public speaking experience and people skills could make a difference in couples' lives. Not long after joining Elevate's officiant team, I realized how much I loved shaping ceremonies that highlight the heart of a couple's journey together. A year later, I took over the business, diving fully into creating memorable ceremonies for couples on their wedding day.

My goal as an officiant is more than just helping a couple exchange vows; I'm here to help them create a memory. Couples may not recall every word spoken, but they'll remember how they felt. And there's only one chance to get it right, to set the perfect tone. I think of this role as capturing a part of their story, even creating a permanent record of it—a beautiful thought for a hobby genealogist like me.

Types of Wedding Ceremonies and Customization Options

Before coming to me, couples have considered the type of wedding ceremony they desire, so let's review the four primary types:

1. Church Ceremony

- **Overview:** A church ceremony takes place within a house of worship and is typically conducted by a minister, priest, or rabbi. Rooted in tradition, these ceremonies often follow a specific religious structure.

- **Customization:** While some church ceremonies allow for personalization, options are often more limited to align with religious traditions. Certain readings, prayers, or musical choices may be permitted, but it's less flexible than other ceremony types. For couples who feel a deep connection to their faith, the church setting offers a powerful spiritual foundation.

2. Civil Ceremony

- **Overview:** Civil ceremonies are non-religious and legally binding. They are officiated by a judge, magistrate, or authorized personnel of the court and are often held at a courthouse. They offer a straightforward and secular option.

- **Customization:** Civil ceremonies are brief and focus on the legalities of marriage rather than personal expression. Some officiants may permit personal vows, but customization is usually minimal. Couples seeking a quick, efficient option often choose civil ceremonies for their simplicity.

3. Officiant Ceremony

- **Overview:** This is where our company comes in. An officiant-led ceremony allows for maximum creativity and flexibility, as we're typically ordained through a religious organization or recognized tribe, enabling us to sign the marriage certificate and perform any ceremony style the couple desires—religious, spiritual, secular, or a blend of all three. A friend or family member may act and sign as officiant if legally ordained and allowed by your state.

- **Customization:** With this type, couples can be as creative as they like. We work with couples to shape every aspect of the ceremony, from personal vows and readings to symbolic unity rituals or even adding a touch of humor. This approach is perfect for couples wanting a deeply personalized, intimate ceremony that reflects their unique love story.

4. Self-Solemnizing Ceremony

- **Overview:** In some states, couples can legally "self-solemnize," meaning they marry themselves without an officiant. This can take place almost anywhere, with or without witnesses.

- **Customization:** This type of ceremony allows for full freedom. Couples can create the structure and content entirely on their own, choosing rituals, vows, and elements that hold personal significance. For those who want a completely unique, intimate experience, self-solemnizing offers a profound way to honor their commitment in a personal setting.

Choosing a ceremony type is just the first step in creating a wedding day that truly reflects who the couple is. But regardless of whether a couple opts for a church, civil, officiant-led, or self-solemnizing ceremony, one thing remains the same: the ceremony itself is the heartbeat of the wedding. It's the sacred moment when two people publicly commit to one another—a defining pause that anchors the celebration to something deeper and more profound. While every other part of the day may blend together, the ceremony is crafted to capture the spirit and essence of their love, creating a memory that resonates long after the vows are spoken.

Each ceremony, no matter the type, has the potential to be something memorable. My job as an officiant is to help couples see that they're not just saying "I do"—they're creating a moment that captures their commitment, personalities, and love. For couples who choose a fully customized ceremony, the result is often a blend of laughter, joyful tears, and a feeling of deep connection.

Getting to Know the Couple: The Customization Process

Every couple's love story deserves to be celebrated in a way that feels uniquely them, and our approach starts with a carefully crafted questionnaire designed to draw out their personalities and values.

- **Shared Vision and Values** – We start with questions about the desired level of spirituality, whether they wish to acknowledge loved ones who couldn't attend, and what values they hold for their marriage. This helps us understand their foundational beliefs and guide the tone of the ceremony to something that feels natural and aligned with their values.

- **Their Story** – Next, we ask about how they met, their favorite memories, and the things they love doing together. These details give us a glimpse into their world, helping us weave elements of their life and love story into the ceremony script.

- **Personal Expressions of Love** – Lastly, we ask each person separately to name three things they love about their partner. This final touch allows for beautifully intimate moments within the ceremony—moments that surprise and move not only the guests but also the couple themselves.

These answers give our team a deeper understanding of their relationship, allowing us to design a ceremony script that is authentic, heartfelt, and entirely personal. When couples review the script, they're often moved to tears because it feels so true to who they are. It's no wonder we receive so many reviews saying, *"It's like you've known us for years!"* That feedback is what fuels my personal passion for officiating. It reinforces why I made the leap from corporate executive to wedding officiant: to set the tone for unforgettable moments, preserve love stories, and remind each couple that their love deserves to be celebrated in a way that feels like theirs.

From Questionnaire to Ceremony Script: Making Customization a Reality

This questionnaire isn't just a formality; it's a conversation starter, a reflection tool, and the key to unlocking a ceremony that feels genuine. Here's how we transform these insights into a beautifully customized ceremony:

- **Building the Foundation** – Through each couple's responses, we gain insight into the tone, style, and language that will resonate with them. We use this to establish a foundation that reflects their personality, whether light-hearted and fun or deeply spiritual.

- **Weaving in Their Love Story** – Through stories and shared experiences they've chosen to share, we craft a narrative that celebrates the couple's journey. We're careful to highlight those pivotal moments that make their relationship unique, using the little details they cherish to make the ceremony unmistakably theirs.

- **Personal Vows and Rituals** – Some couples choose to write their own vows, while others may want a more traditional approach. Some opt to do both. Regardless of their choice, we help guide them to vows and unity rituals that feel right for them, allowing them to honor the ceremony in a way that speaks to who they are.

Each ceremony is a reflection of a couple's relationship, shaped by their individual personalities and shared values. Because we've taken the time to understand who they are, the ceremony script often feels deeply familiar to them, as though it's been written by a friend who truly understands them.

Steps to Creating a Meaningful Ceremony

If you're ready to create a ceremony that captures your relationship, here are a few key steps to guide you:

- **Reflect on Your Relationship** – Spend time discussing with your partner the values, memories, and inside jokes that define your relationship. Don't skip this—it's the foundation of a meaningful ceremony.

- **Choose What Matters** – Think about your desired level of spirituality, the traditions that resonate with you, and any special touches you'd like to include. Whether it's a unity ritual, personal vows, or a mention of loved ones, these elements should reflect who you are as a couple.

- **Collaborate Openly** – Work closely with your officiant, and don't hesitate to share your vision. A good officiant will know how to bring that vision to life with sensitivity and creativity.

One of the most beautiful aspects of a wedding ceremony is how deeply it can reflect the unique relationship between the couple. Personalizing elements like readings and unity ceremonies opens doors for meaningful, memorable moments that resonate not just with the couple but with everyone present. Selecting a reading can be as simple as choosing words that resonate, or it can be an opportunity to honor a shared passion, spiritual connection, or favorite author. Whether the couple selects poetry, song lyrics, scripture, or a passage from a favorite book, these words carry significance that touches hearts in a way only language can.

A unity ceremony is a symbolic ritual performed during a wedding ceremony to represent the joining of two individuals or families into one and adds depth to the personalization of a ceremony. It typically takes place after the exchange of vows and rings and serves to highlight the couple's commitment to each other.

The rituals can be traditional such as the lighting of a unity candle together, meaningful, like Stacy and Xavier's Celtic handfasting ceremony, or fun, like Adry and Erika who took hands-on creativity to a new level with a papier-mâché volcano eruption as a metaphor for their ability to conquer life challenges together. For some couples, customizing their ceremony means incorporating not only meaningful words or symbolic actions but also a theme that reflects a shared passion or story. Theme weddings bring an added layer of fun and personality, infusing the ceremony with elements that make it memorable and unique for everyone involved.

I've had the joy of officiating some wonderfully imaginative ceremonies that speak directly to a couple's interests. Sean and Kai, for instance, held their Star Wars-themed wedding on May 4th—a playful nod to the phrase, 'May the Force be with you.' Gisella and Jason, passionate fans of Tolkien, designed a Hobbit-themed celebration held in a rustic lodge that felt like stepping into a medieval castle. Themes like these add an extra layer of excitement, allowing couples to express themselves fully and create lasting memories for both themselves and their guests.

When you prioritize your ceremony, you're investing in a moment that represents the heartbeat of your wedding day—a memory that will feel as personal and profound as the love you share.

If you're looking for ideas for readings, scripture, vows, or unity ceremonies, check out the many resources on our website at www.ElevateWeddingOfficiant.com.

Reflecting on Our Process: Why We Love What We Do

Over the years, I've been lucky enough to work with so many wonderful couples. Each ceremony reminds me why I chose this path and how deeply meaningful these moments are. I've seen how our process—the questionnaire, the reflections, the personal details—makes each ceremony truly unique. It's a joy to see the emotions and memories it creates for each couple.

At the end of the day, a wedding ceremony is more than an event—it's a celebration of love, a promise, and a reflection of all the moments that brought a couple to this point. That's why we do what we do, and it's why every ceremony is a story we're honored to tell.

Kenya Elizabeth Aissa, MS

Owner of Ruby Envy Wellness LLC

https://www.linkedin.com/in/kenya-e-aissa-ms-91463bb6
https://www.facebook.com/ruby.envy.1
https://www.instagram.com/kenyabeewrites/
https://www.rubyenvywellness.com/
https://www.patreon.com/everythingkenya

Kenya E. Aissa, MS, is an author and the owner of Ruby Envy Wellness LLC. After earning her Master's Degree in Counseling Psychology, she chose to serve the children and families of her community by working as a counselor and social worker for over 20 years before leaning into her true entrepreneurial spirit. Kenya is a yoga teacher and trainer (E-RYT, RYT-500, YACEP), workshop facilitator, and dancer specializing in healing through movement. Kenya's experience as a women's trauma counselor and spirituality group facilitator led to her first book, "Sacred Girl: Spiritual Life Skills for Conscious Young Women", and her second book, "Independent Wife", is scheduled to be released in 2025. Kenya is the co-host of the San Francisco Bay Area radio show, "The Anything Can Happen Show" on 96.9 KGPC.

Mindful Radiance: A Bride's Guide to the Breath/Beauty Connection

By Kenya Elizabeth Aissa, MS

Weddings are a whirlwind of excitement, joy, and sometimes, more than a touch of anxiety. As the big day approaches, brides often find themselves juggling countless details, from floral arrangements to seating charts to managing difficult family members. Amidst this chaos, one essential aspect can be overlooked: The importance of a peaceful atmosphere during the skin prep and makeup application process. In the days, weeks, and months leading up to the wedding day, I make sure my brides focus on skincare, staying hydrated, and minimizing inflammation so that their best skin shines through. However, even if a bride preps like a rockstar, it's important to acknowledge that the mind/body connection includes the largest organ of the body, her skin. There is a profound connection between breathwork and beauty, and there are practical techniques for brides and their makeup artists to cultivate a serene environment that enhances not just their physical appearance, but also their emotional well-being on this momentous occasion.

As an award-winning, internationally published makeup artist, I have seen brides experience a vast spectrum of feelings, from giddy with excitement to so stressed out that they couldn't stop crying. Imagine how challenging it is for the artist to apply makeup to a weeping bride! Even the most expensive waterproof mascara or longwear foundation isn't equipped to survive a bride who is struggling to regulate her emotions on the most important day of her life. Don't forget, photos are forever. Every bride wants to be able to look at her wedding pictures, 10 or 20 years from now, and not see puffy eyes and a swollen face. A peaceful bride means a smooth canvas, fewer touch-ups for the artist, and beautiful photos for the bride. Therefore, it is important that a bride and her MUA, or whoever is the designated head of her beauty team, are in sync. One way to achieve a harmonious application is through breathwork, something that I practice with every bride. Sometimes, it begins with simply creating a safe space between myself and my bride, and mindful breathing is an organic progression of the process.

The Power of Breath

Breathing is a fundamental aspect of life, yet it often goes unnoticed. As a 500-hour RYT and certified trauma-informed yoga teacher, I often have to remind my students to just breathe! As humans, we are literally not getting enough oxygen into our lungs. In moments of stress or excitement, or during traumatic periods of life, our breath can become shallow or rapid, reflecting our emotional state. Conversely, deep, intentional breathing can ground us, calm our minds, and create a sense of peace. In fact, studies show that the psychophysiological effects of breathwork surpass the effects of meditation when it comes to minimizing anxiety and improving mood. Let's take a look at the science of breath, exploring how it impacts our physical and mental health, and sets the stage for why brides should consider incorporating conscious breathing on their wedding day.

The Science of Breath

Deep breathing activates the parasympathetic nervous system, which helps to reduce stress levels, lower blood pressure, and promote relaxation. Furthermore, focusing on the breath helps to clear mental clutter, enhance focus, and increase overall well-being, all things that are critical on the day that you choose to make a lifelong commitment to your partner.

Anxiety is a very common feeling on your wedding day. No one can predict the level of anxiety that one might experience once the day arrives, or what unforeseen circumstances may occur, such as flowers not arriving on time, Aunt Beth having one too many glasses of champagne and having an emotional meltdown while slow dancing with an imaginary partner, or the best man misplacing the ring. Don't worry, these things are NOT likely to happen! But if they do, it's important to have a tool in your emotional arsenal that is a holistic boost to your mental health.

I once had a very sweet bride who was beside herself with worry on her wedding day. I was trying to do her makeup, but she was crying inconsolably. She feared that her fiancé wouldn't show up, that he would realize at the last minute that he didn't love her, and the list went on. Her doctor had prescribed her anti-anxiety medication, as she was prone to overwhelm and emotional dysregulation during stressful times. She suggested that I just keep her pills nearby, and give them to her as she spiraled. Instead, I held her hands and spoke to her in soothing tones, reassuring her that all was well, that her fiancé did indeed adore her, and that he was on his way. I told her to focus her eyes on a part of my shirt, and breathe in through her nose for 7 counts, hold it for 4 counts, and release the breath through her mouth for 10 counts. She was able to quiet her racing thoughts by connecting to her breath. This particular breathing sequence is a wonderful tool to help brides regulate their emotions, gain clarity about their true feelings, and process any lingering apprehensions so that they can embrace the joy of the day.

Peace Within When There's Chaos Without

Creating a calming atmosphere is vital for fostering the kind of internal harmony that every bride deserves as they embark upon their new life. Truly, the bride's energy sets the tone for the entire day, and if she is relaxed and confident, everyone around her will be, too. There are a few tried and true ways that the bride and the makeup artist can collaborate to establish a serene environment that promotes relaxation, and, therefore, a more easeful process of applying makeup.

Setting the Scene

The bride should communicate her wishes regarding the mood that she wants during her beauty prep. Keep in mind that your personality doesn't always align with how you want your "getting ready" space to look or feel! Even the most gregarious bride may feel more comfortable in a semi-controlled environment. Opt for a spot in the room that feels peaceful and inviting. Natural light, soft colors, and minimal clutter can contribute to a calming environment. Should the bride choose to invite her excited squad into the space, she can. However, if she wants a little space, even a corner can be adequate, as long as there is enough room for the beauty team to set up their products and tools, and move around comfortably.

Consider incorporating aromatherapy into the space, being mindful of any sensitivities or potential allergies of the bridal and beauty team. Also, music is magical. It can profoundly influence our mood, and conversely, our mood can dictate what style of music we want to listen to. Therefore, I recommend that every bride have 2 separate playlists during beauty prep. This is definitely a task that I recommend be delegated to someone other than the bride! She's got enough on her plate, right? One of her friends, cousins, or bridesmaids who knows her best should take on this responsibility. Create a playlist of calming tunes, worship music, or nature sounds that help foster tranquility, and also a playlist that's more of a celebratory "party mix". That way, the bride can share what kind of mood she wants her environment to convey, and it'll be ready to go.

The Role of the Makeup Artist

Even though the act of giving and receiving beauty services is often a business transaction, there's no denying that examining someone's skin and touching their face is an intimate experience. A successful beauty session begins with a connection. The makeup artist should take time to engage with the bride, asking her about her feelings and expectations for the day. By closely listening to the bride's thoughts and concerns, the makeup artist can tailor the experience to meet her needs. The MUA can speak with the bride's support people, such as her bridesmaids, her mother, or an aunt, and gently guide them towards things they can do to be helpful. This is also an exciting day for family and friends, and they may get carried away while they're sipping on pre-ceremony flutes of champagne. A great time should be had by all, but sometimes it's left to the MUA to curate the environment and rein people in for the sake of the bride's peace. As the makeup artist applies each product, they can incorporate breathwork techniques to facilitate the bride's experience of relaxation and release: mind, body, and spirit relaxation, and release of fears, anxieties, and the need to control wedding day minutiae. Here are some classic breathwork techniques that can be used to help the bride manage her stress on her wedding day, and beyond.

Diaphragmatic Breathing

Diaphragmatic breathing, also known as abdominal or deep breathing, is a powerful technique that can significantly enhance physical and mental well-being. This method engages the diaphragm, allowing for deeper inhalation and exhalation, which promotes relaxation and improves overall lung function.

One of the most notable benefits of diaphragmatic breathing is its ability to reduce stress and anxiety fairly quickly. When we are stressed, our bodies tend to engage in shallow, rapid breathing, or "hyperventilating", which can lead to even greater anxiety, dizziness, or feeling like we're going to faint. By practicing deep breathing, we activate the body's relaxation response, triggering the release of endorphins and lowering cortisol levels. This shift can lead to a calmer state of mind, as well as smooth, relaxed facial muscles, a perfect canvas for the artist.

How to practice diaphragmatic breathing:

1. Sit or lie down in a comfortable position. If sitting, keep your back straight and your feet flat on the floor. If lying down, place

your arms at your sides, on your belly, or one hand on your heart and the other on your belly.
2. Take a deep breath through your nose. Focus on expanding your abdomen, allowing your diaphragm to move down and your belly to rise. Aim to keep your chest relatively still.
3. Once you've inhaled fully, hold your breath for a moment (about 2–5 seconds), allowing the oxygen to saturate your bloodstream.
4. Exhale slowly and completely through your mouth and nose. Focus on the feeling of your abdomen falling as you release the air.
5. Continue this process for 5–10 minutes, gradually increasing the duration as you become more comfortable with the technique.

Box Breathing

Box breathing, also known as square breathing, is a simple yet profound technique that helps regulate the breath and calm the mind. This practice involves inhaling, holding, exhaling, and pausing for equal counts, creating a "box" pattern. Box breathing is widely used by athletes, military personnel, and those in high-stress professions. One of the primary benefits is its ability to reduce stress and anxiety levels. By consciously controlling the breath, individuals can activate the parasympathetic nervous system, which induces a state of calm and relaxation. This is particularly beneficial in high-pressure situations, as it helps to ground the individual and restore a sense of control.

Box breathing supports emotional regulation, and can help people to observe their thoughts and feelings without judgment. Over time, this practice can increase emotional resilience, and the ability to respond to even the most challenging situations, with a "whoo-sahhhhh" state of mind.

How to practice box breathing:

1. Sit or lie down in a comfortable position. Ensure your back is straight and your shoulders are relaxed.
2. Gently close your eyes to minimize distractions and help focus your attention inward.
3. Slowly inhale through your nose for a count of four. Focus on filling your lungs completely and expanding your abdomen.
4. Once you've inhaled fully, hold your breath for another count of four. During this pause, allow your body to relax and focus your thoughts on the breath.
5. Exhale slowly through your mouth for a count of four. Concentrate on the sensation of the air leaving your lungs as you empty them fully.
6. After exhaling, hold your breath again for a count of four. Use this time to feel the calmness enveloping you.
7. Continue this cycle for several minutes, gradually increasing the duration over time as you become more comfortable with the practice.

Nadi Shodhana

My favorite breathing technique, Nadi Shodhana, is the first thing that I taught my fellow students during my yoga teacher training final exam. Nadi Shodana is alternate nostril breathing and a powerful pranayama technique rooted in ancient yogic traditions. This practice involves breathing through one nostril at a time, balancing the left and right hemispheres of the brain. This can enhance cognitive function, improve focus, promote harmony within the body and mind, and increase overall productivity. Furthermore, this technique is believed to help balance the body's energy channels, or "nadis". According to yogic philosophy, blocked energy can lead to physical and emotional imbalances. Nadi Shodhana helps to clear these blockages, promoting a smooth flow of prana (life force) throughout the body. All of these benefits are a valuable addition to any bride's wellness toolbox and can help our bride step into married life as her best, most vibrant self.

How to practice Nadi Shodhana:

1. Sit in a comfortable position, keeping in mind what is available to your body; for example, cross-legged on the floor or seated in a chair with your feet flat on the floor. Keep your spine straight, and your shoulders relaxed.
2. Using your right hand, fold your index and middle fingers toward your palm, leaving your thumb and ring finger extended. Your thumb will be used to close the right nostril, and the ring finger will close the left.
3. With your right thumb, gently close your right nostril. Inhale deeply and slowly through your left nostril for a count of four, filling your lungs completely.
4. At the top of your inhalation, close your left nostril with your ring finger, and release your right nostril. Exhale slowly through your right nostril for a count of four, allowing any tension to leave your body.
5. Inhale through your right nostril for a count of four. At the top of your inhalation, close your right nostril with your thumb, and release your left nostril.
6. Exhale through your left nostril for a count of four.
7. Repeat the cycle. Continue this alternating pattern for 3–5 minutes, or whatever is comfortable, focusing on your breath and the sensations in your body.

Incorporating any of these breathwork techniques before, during, and after the wedding can help the bride with stress management, mental clarity, and emotional stability. By taking just a few moments to focus on your breath, you can cultivate a sense of peace and control in your life, and there's no better time to learn these skills than when preparing for one of life's most beautiful, and most challenging, journeys. Yes, it's important to live in this moment, enjoy the day, and not "future-trip". However, stress-reduction and mindfulness techniques will stay with the bride throughout her life—when she's no longer a bride, but a wife, mom, employee, business owner, or whatever life brings her. Walking this life with your love is one of life's most intense adventures. We can safely assume that hard days may come when we will question not only our choices but our very sanity. It's wise to have every possible skill at our disposal so that we can meet those challenges head-on, knowing that our body's response to stressful stimuli is under our control.

The Calm Before the Ceremony

As the sun rises on a wedding day, a flurry of emotions envelops the bride. Excitement, anticipation, and perhaps a tinge of anxiety swirl within her. In the midst of the hustle and bustle, carving out time for quiet reflection can ground the bride. Before the whirlwind of the day begins, find a tranquil space—perhaps a corner in the bridal suite or even a quiet garden. Sit comfortably, close your eyes, and take a few deep breaths. Inhale deeply through the nose, allowing the breath to fill the belly, and exhale slowly through the mouth. This simple act of focusing on the breath can help center the mind, calm the body, and set a tone of appreciation for the day ahead.

Practicing Gratitude

Many years ago, there was a sign at my place of employment that read: "Put Some Gratitude In Your Attitude!" I thought it was kind of ironically funny at the time because, after a grueling hour-and-a-half-long commute, the first thing I saw upon entering the building was that sign! However, I realized that gratitude is not simply a byproduct of favorable circumstances; it is an active choice. It encourages us to acknowledge the blessings in our lives, and not just focus on the annoying inconveniences, complicated relationships, and fears that encroach upon our lives. I may have had a terrible commute, but I had a job that I loved, where I was appreciated, and where I experienced incredible personal and professional growth. By remembering to practice gratitude, we learn to savor experiences, creating a ripple effect that spreads throughout every aspect of our lives. Ultimately, the power of gratitude lies in its ability to illuminate the beauty in our lives, highlighting the people and experiences that bring us joy. On a day that's overflowing with every possible feeling, gratitude can shift the bride's mindset from overwhelm to appreciation. Before stepping into her wedding dress, she might take a moment to incorporate some of the above breathing techniques into a tangible practice or tradition. For example, the sweet tradition of writing a love note to her partner. Breathing in clarity, and breathing out her hopes, dreams, and commitments onto the page can serve as a reminder of the love that underpins the coming ceremony.

Grounding

On my wedding day 22 years ago, I was hit with two unexpected pieces of bad news prior to the ceremony: one, my makeup artist backed out at the last minute, and two, one of my best friends got into a huge fight with her husband and wasn't coming. I had been counting on both of these people for very different reasons, and both of them were important pieces of my mental wellness puzzle on my big day. Instead of feeling relaxed, I felt untethered and anxious. My close friend Alana stepped in to help settle me down. She was a soothing voice of reason, reminding me that although I would have preferred to have someone else do my makeup, this was a mere inconvenience. I was, in fact, a makeup artist, and, therefore, fully capable of doing the job myself. She also reminded me that this day was a reflection of real life, where people are unpredictable and going through their own stuff. She said that this was a perfect opportunity to practice pivoting to a different mindset, since I would most likely have a long future ahead of me where things are simply not going to go my way. As the ceremony approached, staying grounded became crucial. Alana taught me a grounding exercise that was a lifesaver and set the tone for the rest of the day. The 5-4-3-2-1 grounding exercise helped me to remain anchored in the "now", rather than slowly spiraling under the knowledge that some things had gotten out of my control. The truth was, neither the makeup artist nor my friend was ever in my control, to begin with. Once I did the exercise, I was able to release my negative feelings of hurt and disappointment, and instead, focus on the people who had shown up. I peacefully applied my own makeup to a face that wasn't pinched from tension.

Here is how a bride can lead herself in the 5-4-3-2-1 grounding technique:

- Five things you can see: Take a moment to admire your flowers, the loving smiles of your friends and family, or the landscape right outside of your bridal suite.
- Four things you can feel: The soft fabric of your dress, the carpet under your feet, the warmth of the sun, or the chilly condensation on a glass of water.
- Three things you can hear: Music! Laughter! Glasses clinking!
- Two things you can smell: Your own perfume, maybe even the sweet baby scent of a niece or nephew.
- One thing you can taste: A sip of champagne or a bite of something sweet, savoring the flavors on your tongue.

This exercise not only grounds the bride in the present but also enhances her appreciation for the day unfolding around her. These moments only happen once, and our memories of many things, no matter how precious, will eventually fade. Using all of her senses to experience these moments with gratitude will help embed the memories in the bride's heart for a lifetime.

In this fast-paced world, the simple act of breathing can be a powerful tool for connection. As you embark on your wedding journey, let your breath serve as a reminder of the beauty that lies within you—both inside and out.

Ashley McCombs

Founder of Lemon Ivory Beauty
Luxury Hair and Makeup Artist

https://www.instagram.com/lemonivorybeauty/
https://lemonivorybeauty.com/

Based in Dallas, Texas, Ashley McCombs is a luxury hair and makeup artist known for creating soft, romantic looks for brides. As the founder of Lemon Ivory Beauty, she focuses on delivering timeless elegance through personalized service and flawless attention to detail. Her artistry reflects a deep understanding of her clients' unique visions, ensuring they look and feel radiant on their most cherished day.

Renowned for her professionalism and dedication to excellence, Ashley McCombs has become a trusted name in the luxury beauty industry, helping clients throughout Dallas, Texas, and beyond feel their most beautiful.

From the First Look to the Last Dance: Why Bridal Hair and Makeup Matter

By Ashley McCombs

In retrospect, my journey to becoming a Luxury Hair and Makeup Artist seemed almost predetermined. I was inspired the moment I understood that beauty is more often created than inherited. Its creation is nothing less than empowering. As Marilyn Monroe once said, "Give a woman the right makeup, and she can conquer the world."

In the neighborhood where I grew up, I can't recall a time when family, friends, and neighbors didn't call me "Little Miss Hollywood." But I earned that nickname not for the reasons you might assume. I wasn't a child who was captivated by celebrities and their lives. I didn't dream of being an actress or walking down the red carpet in front of the paparazzi. I wasn't star-struck.

Instead, I was enchanted by beauty and fashion. I adored glamor. I was fascinated with the subtle art of transformation. From an early age, I realized that hair and makeup were all about self-expression. I desperately wanted to learn all the "secrets" and create magic for myself and those around me. However, it wouldn't be accurate to say that beauty was my passion. Such a claim would be a vast understatement. It became central to my lifestyle and belief that each of us can manifest our future.

I learned and practiced my craft, first with practical experience and then with mentorship. I kept my dream alive even as life presented me with the gift of motherhood. For a time, I became a stay-at-home mom to four wonderful boys: Gates, Briggs, Navys, and Oaks. I love being a mother and certainly didn't regret putting my ambition on hold, but I never gave up on my first dream. As my boys grew older, I could finally turn my talents into something more than passion. I realized that manifesting beauty in others could be the key to building an exciting future for myself—and perhaps inspire my sons to follow their dreams.

So, I went to hair school, advanced my skills, developed my art, and soon began working in a hair salon. At first, it was exciting to have the ability to build a clientele through the power of my own talent. But before long, I found that I was bored with the routine. I was still "Little Miss Hollywood." I wanted to create glamor and make a genuine impact on the self-image of others. I craved grander challenges and clients that would demand the best. I wanted, too, to be able to meet and exceed their expectations and offer them something extraordinary. I also wanted to build a business—to be my own boss and serve a clientele that shares my passion.

For years, I had helped create hair and makeup for free, helping friends and family on special occasions. I relished the excitement and energy of supporting women during special events, like weddings, where all eyes were upon them and where they needed to look their best. I wanted the excitement and frenetic energy that takes your breath away.

I needed to be at the heart of it all and work incessantly toward my objective, even juggling family responsibilities.

Fashion icon Coco Chanel once said, "Caring about beauty, it is necessary to start with the heart and soul." I believe that, too. My choice to become a luxury hair and makeup artist is about so much more than the craft itself. It represents my desire to contribute, innovate, and improve. Simply stated, I seek to create joy; there's no greater feeling when I succeed in that mission.

I welcomed all the obstacles and challenges I faced. When you find a calling, there's nothing else you would rather do, and hard work becomes a pleasure. After volunteering for countless events and working under some of the most talented artists in my business, I decided to take a leap of faith and begin to build my business as a luxury Hair and Makeup Artist.

I have never been happier.

WHERE DO YOU START?

If you're planning a wedding—for yourself or your loved ones—it's essential to realize that you're not simply preparing for a moment in time or a single photograph. By every measurement, a wedding ceremony and reception is a legacy for yourself, your family, and your friends. It will live on in the memory of loved ones for decades. It sets the stage for the future. The moment when the bride and groom take their vows is undoubtedly the highlight, but a wedding is about the entire presentation, including the ceremony and the reception—and more.

A wedding is about preparing for the big day.

For those seeking a memorable affair and willing to put in the time, effort, and, yes, money into producing the ultimate night to remember, "do-it-yourself" is unacceptable. The finest wedding requires a team of professionals at the top of their game to make it happen.

With the assistance of vendors from wedding planners, florists, caterers, photographers, and hair and makeup artists, you can envision and bring to reality an exquisite, life-changing experience and an unforgettable memory that will live on for decades. Cutting corners is not an option.

But sticker shock is real. Weddings are expensive, and there's a temptation to look for places to save. Sometimes, hair and makeup are perceived as a secondary concern. But choose the wrong hair and makeup team, and you risk a fashion faux that will be preserved forever in photos and videos that your children and grandchildren will relive.

Just as a wedding planner and your venue must be booked far in advance, it's never too early to begin looking for a professional, top-quality Hair and Makeup Artist (HMUA). A talented HMUA will make a tangible difference for the bride and her party. This will be another considerable expense, but consider how impactful having an HMUA can be.

A professional Hair and Makeup team allows you to do the unexpected. I enabled a magnificent, gorgeous entrance for one bride. She caused a sensation as she walked down the aisle with stunning Hollywood waves. But that wasn't the highlight of the day. The bride and I had a secret in store. After the ceremony, we retreated to the bridal suite, where I prepared her for the reception. But I wasn't only refreshing her hair and makeup.

I cut off twelve inches of her hair, restyled her appearance, and then she made a second dramatic entrance into the reception. Her fresh look surprised and delighted her guests, and her new husband was nothing less than enchanted by the unexpected results. It was a heartwarming moment that wouldn't have been possible without the right team.

An HMUA's contribution can be magical for reasons that aren't always about the bride. At one wedding, my work with the mother of the bride was especially meaningful. She had suffered for years from the debilitating effects of Parkinson's disease, a brain condition that impacts muscle control. With her fine hand coordination hopelessly compromised, she had long since given up attempting to apply makeup, and generally went without any adornment. But for this special day, she wanted to feel and look her best for her daughter. I applied her makeup and made her dream come true. She sobbed with happiness when she saw the result in the mirror. Maybe I sobbed, too.

A luxury Hair and Makeup Artist is far more than a beauty consultant. She is also part psychologist. When you're looking for the right HMUA, it's essential that you find someone with a calm demeanor and understanding that puts you at ease and doesn't intimidate you into making decisions you might later regret. Hair and makeup at a wedding aren't tasks to be checked off a "to-do" list. They're key to creating the experience. Weddings are unavoidably chaotic. Countless brides are tempted every day to throw up their hands and call the whole thing off. A bride must have a safe space to cool off, transform, and re-energize. An HMUA will form that cocoon.

In the intense stress leading up to that Big Moment, brides sometimes need to vent their emotions away from family and friends. As we prepared for one wedding, the bride told me, "Please keep my mother away. She's not allowed in this room." She didn't hate her mother, but as we all know, mother-daughter dynamics can be complicated, especially at a wedding. In addition to my traditional responsibilities, it became my instant obligation to keep peace in the family. I had to creatively navigate the situation, informing her mother, very gently, to "give us a few minutes," and insisting (almost like a diva) that I preferred to work privately and couldn't tolerate anyone else in the room distracting me. For the record, I'm usually more flexible in those situations, but my first responsibility was to the bride, so I temporarily took on a new persona. I was careful not to offend the mother or share her daughter's secret desire to keep her out of the room, but instead, I smoothed over the tense moments so that they avoided a crisis and everyone could remain calm. Maybe the mother of the bride was a little frustrated, but all was forgotten when her daughter emerged, ready to make her entrance.

Your HMUA should become an integral part of your team, and you need to consider the right strategy to work with them effectively. Professional HMUAs understand that they are there to offer advice and apply their experience to fulfill your wishes. You'll set the rules, but the relationship shouldn't be adversarial. It's not a competition. It's a collaboration.

In a Hollywood movie, hair and makeup are just as crucial to the production as the actors, the camera, lighting, and special effects.

Without proper hair and makeup, the director's vision and the work of the rest of the team are compromised. If all of the elements of the production are not the best they can possibly be—if the lighting isn't right or if the performances are lacking—the production will be ruined and the vision lost forever. Like a wedding, one poorly executed element in a movie, even hair and makeup, can ruin the entire experience for the audience. And just like a wedding, that mistake or oversight will be preserved for a long time.

Hair and makeup should be one of your earliest considerations when planning a wedding. Well-meaning friends and family might confidently offer advice or assistance to help you save some money, but while they have scattered experience, they're not professionals. They likely won't have the know-how to provide the right advice or have the temperament to work under pressure on the day of your event. They might find themselves overwhelmed but choose to keep silent out of loyalty to you and a reluctance to admit when they're in over their heads. If you place a friend in that position, your friendship may not survive the wedding.

Sometimes, there's a perception that applying hair and makeup for a wedding isn't much different than hair and makeup for a dinner party. A genuine HMUA, however, doesn't just want to help you look "good." She will transform you, make you look glamorous, and make sure that you photograph well. Once the wedding is over and everyone goes home, your photos and video will be all you have left, so amazing hair and makeup is a priceless legacy.

Friends can sometimes help you look good, but they don't have the training and insight to make you look amazing.

DO YOUR RESEARCH AND CHOOSE CAREFULLY

Start searching early for your HMUA so that you have the opportunity to book the best artists for your wedding. I'm booked with some clients a year or more in advance.

While it's not always possible, it's best to begin planning for your wedding nine to eighteen months before the wedding. If you don't have that long, don't panic—just be prepared to accelerate your decisions and act quickly.

Remember, looking for a bargain when hiring a Hair and Makeup Artist for your wedding is like going for a balayage. You can be certain you'll need color correction and spend twice the money to fix the mistakes.

If you opt for a luxury HMUA—a top-quality industry professional—you should expect to pay at least $200 for each person in your party. Your Artist has invested thousands of dollars in education, training, experience, and extensive product knowledge. She'll use high-end products and is insured. You're likely to find many pretenders that charge much less and claim to offer more, but you can be assured of one thing: you get what you pay for. You deserve better, especially for your wedding!

A luxury HMUA will focus on the details. They'll think of issues you may not have considered and understand to solve problems. They'll make sure that your lipstick doesn't begin to flake off mid-ceremony and that you have a quality waterproof mascara that won't streak down your face as you tearfully recite your vows. If you ever seen that happen, you know it's not a pretty sight!

The right HMUA will be familiar with all the latest wedding trends and tricks to achieve the best results. They will have the experience to create a look that will last throughout the entire ten- or sixteen-hour day and stand by to help you.

But how do you find the right artist?

That might be when fear of the unknown grips you, and you might be tempted to follow the now time-honored path of calling on the social media "hive mind," putting out a public call for recommendations on

Facebook and elsewhere. Responses will surely come pouring in from every direction—but how can you possibly wade through a hundred potential vendors? Seeking community recommendations might be a good strategy for a house painter but not for the best Hair and Makeup Artists.

Before you throw out the net and hope to catch the right fish, look in your own proverbial backyard. Turn first to people you know and trust—your intimate network—family, friends, and colleagues who could have firsthand knowledge of luxury HMUAs that might be perfect for your wedding. You're starting your search with three to five candidates that already come highly recommended by people you know. You can always expand your search later.

Now that you have some names, do some initial research. Google them, check the images they post on Instagram Check their websites. Read customer reviews. How does their overall image feel to you? Do they seem to have the experience to create the look you desire? You're not making a decision at this point, but you can gain an initial sense of a potential match.

Next, send them an inquiry, including as much detail as you can offer—dates, the size of the party, and your expectations before and during the event. Include your budgetary limitations. Evaluate their initial response to you. Their first response should be friendly, informative, and respectful. It should demonstrate that they have read your material. If you like what you see and the tone of their response, then move to the next step and schedule a consultation.

Professional, reputable HMUAs are happy to offer a free consultation call. Remember that a consult is not meant to be a sales pitch; it's an opportunity to listen and interact, ask questions, and determine if the HMUA is a good match. Do they have the mindset and the sense of style that compliments your vision? Do they sync with your personality?

Their initial behavior is an early indicator of the experience you will have later. A professional understands that a consult is nothing less than an audition.

When you're getting ready for your consultation, read the material the HMUA sent you, and make sure to find ample time and a quiet place to have an active conversation.

Establishing trust is essential. Don't be intimidated. A reputable HMUA can handle constructive criticism without getting defensive. You should feel comfortable about being transparent and honest about your concept for hair and makeup, and feel free to offer your perspective without hesitation. At the same time, you should be open to hearing their ideas and considerate of their suggestions and advice without being offended if you disagree. If your HMUA is a reputable professional, she will be skilled at putting you at ease and finding the right compromise.

Once you're ready to make a decision and choose your HMUA, don't wait. Move quickly to put down a deposit, sign a contract, and reserve your desired date. A verbal promise is never enough! Top-notch HMUAs are booked far in advance, and you need to guarantee they will be available. Keep in mind that prime dates (Fridays, Saturdays, and Holidays) are booked early and can be hard to find at the last minute. Move quickly to lock in your Dream Team.

Expect and accept that you will pay a premium for the best people—but recognize that you're paying for their expertise, professionalism, product quality, travel expense, glam, and sophistication. If you've done research and chosen well, you'll have the comfort and security of knowing that you're working with one of the best HMUAs in your area.

GETTING READY, STRESS-FREE!

The booking, of course, is only the beginning.

As the wedding day approaches, there are steps you can take to make sure you're prepared for your HMUA. Until the event, your carefully chosen HMUA will be your resource and guide. They want you to succeed and be completely satisfied. They are invested in your happiness and your best interests. Your success is their success.

Keep in mind that:

1. Every hair and makeup artist has different preferences in regard to the time and physical space they need to deliver their best work. If you have a larger wedding party, consider booking a hotel conference room or even an AirBnB in addition to the Bridal Suite. The hotel might not let you into a bridal suite early enough, and you'll want to keep the suite clean and orderly for staged photos. In a separate space, you can relax with the other members of your party, maybe sip on a mimosa, listen to your favorite music, and enjoy those last special moments with your girls!

2. The larger your party, the more time your Hair and Makeup team needs to prepare everyone in time for the wedding. Trust your HMUA. With first looks, first touches, and an array of bridal portraits, you'll need to be ready much earlier than you might expect. Remember, the ceremony itself isn't the deadline. Your HMUA wants you to enjoy every moment of the preparation process and will plan accordingly. No one likes stress!

3. Follow your HMUA's advance prep instructions so that you and your "bride tribe" arrive on the day of the wedding with skin perfectly prepped for a flawless result. To have flawless makeup, prioritize quality skincare well in advance. Pay attention to your

makeup artist's recommendations for an effective skincare routine and follow it religiously leading up to your wedding day. Listen to their advice! They've dealt with every challenge in skincare and will know what to do in your case, too.

4. Don't expect to book individual appointments for the convenience of each member of your bridal party. Arrange for everyone to assemble at the beginning of your hair and makeup session so that the process can move without delay and everyone will be ready when the time comes. Some people will take longer than others, so the timeline can be unpredictable. Everyone should be in place and ready to take their turn as soon as they're asked.

5. Prepare your robes, dresses, and photography details the night before so that on your wedding day, all you have left to do is enjoy the experience. You need to do your part so the HMUA can do their part.

CONCLUSION

Families spend more money on weddings today than ever before. Part of the reason, according to numerous informal surveys, is that some people simply want to show off. I don't believe that's the only explanation.

Whether or not you use social media, peering into the lives of others has made us collectively interested in "keeping up" and creating an unforgettable experience for our guests. We want to put on a good show simply because that's what we see on social media—everyone around us is putting on a show, and now it's our turn. While that might sound trite, there's yet another motivation to consider.

I believe that many couples sincerely want their guests to have a good time and feel as happy and excited as they do. They want to do their best to entertain and thrill everyone in the wedding party.

A hair and makeup team should share your passion for creating joy. They'll be at least as passionate about your hair and makeup as you are about your new beginning.

Your HMUA should have one objective, and it's precisely the same as I had when I was "Little Miss Hollywood."

To make magic happen.

Candice Damele

Founder of Damele Bridal
Bridal Styling Expert

https://www.facebook.com/DameleBridal
https://www.instagram.com/damelebridal/
https://damelebridal.com/

Candice Damele is the passionate owner of Damele Bridal, a boutique dedicated to providing brides with a personalized and memorable shopping experience. After facing unexpected challenges, including a major rebranding and a diagnosis of multiple sclerosis, Candice transformed her vision into a thriving business. With a curated selection of bridal gowns, she excels at helping brides find the perfect dress that reflects their unique style. Despite operating from a cozy 900 sq ft space, her boutique has gained recognition as one of the best in the Dallas-Fort Worth area, earning multiple accolades and featuring on CBS Destination Dallas. Candice believes in the importance of quality, personal attention, and fostering a warm, intimate atmosphere for brides and their loved ones. Her commitment to making each bride feel beautiful and special on their big day is the driving force behind Damele Bridal, where every appointment is a private and educational journey toward finding the perfect gown.

Unveiling the Perfect Gown: Smart Strategies for Stress-Free Dress Shopping

By Candice Damele

Shopping for a wedding dress is often portrayed as a magical experience filled with tears of joy and unforgettable moments. However, it can also be a daunting process that, if not approached thoughtfully, may lead to emotional buying and regrets later. This chapter is your go-to guide for prepping for dress appointments, scoring the right boutique, and homing in on your personal style. Plus, we'll chat about why hitting up local brick-and-mortar stores can make your shopping experience not just easier but way more enjoyable. Let's get started and make your dress shopping experience truly memorable!

Prepping for Your Appointment

Before you dive into trying on dresses, a little prep goes a long way. Here's what you should do to ensure you have a great time:

1. **Set a Budget**: First things first, figure out your budget. Wedding dresses typically fall in the range of $1,500 to $3,000, but prices can vary a lot, unless you're considering couture options, which can significantly exceed that range. Do some homework on what local boutiques charge, and don't forget to factor in costs for alterations, accessories (like veils and jewelry), and dress preservation. A good rule of thumb is to set aside about 10-15% of your overall wedding budget for the dress itself. And hey, it's totally fine to have a little wiggle room if you find a dress that really speaks to you.

   If you're working with a tighter budget, consider looking for sample dresses. Many boutiques offer discounts on sample gowns—these are the dresses that were used for try-ons and fashion shows. You can snag a beautiful dress at a fraction of the price, often 30-50% off retail. Just keep in mind that these dresses may require some alterations to ensure the perfect fit, but they can be a fantastic way to get a designer gown without breaking the bank.

2. **Do Your Research**: Spend some time scrolling through bridal magazines, Pinterest, and social media to gather inspiration. Save some pictures of dresses you love, but keep an open mind—sometimes, what looks amazing in a photo doesn't always work in real life.

3. **Select Your Entourage Wisely and Know It's Okay to Say Yes by Yourself**: Choose a small group of supportive people to come with you. Too many voices can cloud your judgment, so pick those whose opinions you trust and who will cheer you on.

    However, don't feel pressured to have a whole squad around you to make a decision. If you find a dress that makes you feel like a queen, go for it—even if your entourage isn't fully on board. You're the one wearing it, and your happiness is what matters most. It's perfectly acceptable to say yes to a dress on your own or even the same day you try it on. If you feel a connection with a dress, trust your instincts and commit; waiting too long could mean that gorgeous gown gets discontinued!

4. **Make Appointments in Advance**: Many bridal boutiques work on an appointment-only basis, so call ahead and snag a time that works for you.

5. **Trust the Stylist**: The stylists at the boutique are your best friends in this process. They know what works for different body types and styles, so don't be afraid to share your vision with them. They might suggest something you wouldn't have picked out yourself, and you could end up loving it!

6. **Communicate Openly**: As you try on dresses, be honest about how you feel about each one. If something doesn't feel right or you just don't love it, let your stylist know. This feedback is essential for them to help you find dresses that really match your style.

   And if you have any sensory issues—like sensitivity to certain fabrics—definitely mention that upfront. The stylist can help steer you toward options that won't make you uncomfortable. If you have specific goals related to your body or any concerns about how a dress might fit in the future, don't hesitate to share them with your stylist. They are there to support you and can help find options that make you feel comfortable and confident, no matter where you are in your journey!

7. **Consider Wearing Proper Shapewear**: The right shapewear can make a big difference in how a dress fits and feels. It's worth investing in a good-quality shapewear piece that smooths and supports your body, enhancing your silhouette without sacrificing comfort. Whether you prefer a bodysuit, high-waisted briefs, or a slip, make sure to try on shapewear with the dresses you're considering to see how they work together. It can help you achieve the look you want and ensure you feel great throughout your special day.

8. **Alterations Are Key**: Remember that alterations are an additional cost to factor into your budget, but they're absolutely essential for achieving the perfect fit. A skilled tailor can transform a dress into something that looks like it was made just for you. Whether it's taking in the waist, shortening the hem, or adjusting the neckline, alterations can make all the difference in how the dress fits and feels on your big day. So, budget for this important step to ensure you look and feel your best!

9. **Ask About Taking Photos**: Don't hesitate to ask if you can take some pictures while trying on dresses. It can be super helpful to look

at your options from a different perspective. Just remember: a quick snap with your cell phone won't capture the magic of how you'll look in professional wedding photos. So, keep in mind that the lighting, angles, and overall vibe can be very different on the big day!

Knowing It's Not the Dress

Sometimes, despite the excitement, a dress just doesn't feel right. Here are some signs to help you recognize when it might be time to move on:

1. **Nit-Picking**: If you find yourself constantly pointing out small flaws or wishing for major changes to make the dress fit your vision, it might not be the one for you. A dress should make you feel fabulous as it is and not require a laundry list of alterations to meet your expectations.

2. **Making Tons of Changes**: If you're envisioning a dress that needs significant alterations or adjustments—like a complete redesign of the silhouette, neckline, or train—it may be a sign that this dress isn't meant for you. While minor tweaks are normal, if you're trying to change the essence of the dress, it's worth reconsidering.

3. **Comparing to Other Dresses**: If you find yourself comparing the dress you're trying on to a previous dress you loved, that might indicate it's not living up to your expectations. Every dress has its unique charm, and if you're stuck in your head about another gown, it may be a signal to keep looking for something that truly captures your heart.

4. **Trusting Your Instincts**: Pay attention to how you feel when wearing the dress. If you're experiencing any doubt or discomfort, don't ignore those feelings. Your wedding dress should evoke joy and confidence, so if you're not feeling it, trust that instinct and keep exploring other options.

5. **Physical Movements**: Be aware of your body language when trying on dresses. If you find yourself fidgeting, adjusting constantly, or unable to stand still, it could indicate that the dress isn't right for you. On the flip side, if you catch yourself swaying or moving with ease, it's a good sign that you're low-key in love with that dress!

The Value of Investing in a Quality Wedding Dress

When it comes to wedding dresses, investing in a quality gown from a local boutique can make all the difference. Here's why:

1. **Craftsmanship and Quality Materials**: Local boutiques often carry dresses made from high-quality fabrics with superior craftsmanship. These dresses are designed to fit well and last, ensuring that you not only look stunning on your big day but also feel comfortable. Quality materials will also wear better over time, giving you peace of mind as you move and dance throughout the day.

2. **Personalized Experience**: Shopping at a local boutique provides you with a personalized experience that online shopping simply cannot match. You have the opportunity to try on dresses, receive tailored advice from knowledgeable stylists, and enjoy a fitting experience that is all about you. This personalized attention helps ensure that you find a dress that reflects your unique style and personality.

3. **Supporting Local Economy**: By investing in a local boutique, you are supporting small businesses in your community. This contributes to the local economy and fosters a sense of connection within your area. Plus, many local boutiques offer exclusive designs and unique selections that you may not find anywhere else.

4. **Avoiding the Pitfalls of Cheap Online Options**: While it may be tempting to save money by purchasing a cheaper dress online, there are significant risks involved. Dresses bought online often lack the same quality of materials and construction as those from reputable boutiques. Sizing can be inconsistent, leading to a frustrating experience when the dress doesn't fit as expected.

Additionally, alterations can often cost more than the dress itself when purchasing from online retailers, especially if the fit is far from what you need. Many brides find that once they factor in the cost of alterations to correct poor fit or design issues from cheap online dresses, they end up spending more than if they had invested in a quality gown from the start. The return process can also be complicated, leaving you in a tough spot as your wedding day approaches.

Investing in a quality dress from a local boutique means you'll have a gown that not only looks beautiful but is also made to last, enhancing your overall wedding experience.

Finding the Right Boutique

Not all bridal shops are the same, so let's find one that vibes with your style:

1. **Local vs. Chain Stores**: Go for local boutiques whenever possible. They usually offer a more personal experience, with staff who genuinely want to help you find the perfect dress. Plus, supporting local businesses is always a win!

2. **Research Boutique Specialties**: Different shops carry different styles. Some might focus on modern designs, while others have a great selection of vintage or plus-size options. Check out their websites or social media to see what they have in stock.

3. **Read Reviews**: Take a peek at customer reviews to get a feel for others' experiences. Positive feedback about the boutique's atmosphere and staff can help you narrow down your choices.

4. **Visit in Advance**: If you can, pop into a few boutiques without the pressure of an appointment. This way, you can see how the staff interacts with customers and what kind of dresses they have.

Configuring Your Aesthetic

Nailing down your wedding dress style is super important and can significantly narrow down your options. Here's why defining your aesthetic helps you find the best wedding dress:

1. **Identify Your Personal Style**: Think about your everyday wardrobe. What makes you feel confident? Use that as a guide to help determine your bridal style—whether it's classic, bohemian, modern, or vintage. Understanding your personal style will make it easier to spot dresses that resonate with you and eliminate those that don't feel right.

2. **Consider Your Wedding Theme**: Your dress should fit the overall vibe of your wedding. A beach wedding might call for something more relaxed, while a formal evening ceremony might need a classic ball gown. By aligning your dress choice with your wedding theme, you can create a cohesive look that enhances the overall experience.

3. **Prioritize Comfort**: While it's easy to get swept up in how a dress looks, comfort is key. Make sure you can move freely and feel good in whatever you choose. A dress that reflects your aesthetic but feels uncomfortable will only hinder your confidence on your big day.

4. **Create a Mood Board**: Put together a mood board with dress inspirations, color palettes, and fabric swatches. This visual guide can help clarify your preferences and serve as a reference during your shopping.

Lasting Impressions

Wedding dress shopping can be a fun and exciting adventure when you approach it with the right mindset. By setting a budget, researching local boutiques, defining your style, trusting your stylist, communicating openly, and enjoying the personalized service offered by brick-and-mortar stores, you can navigate the process without getting caught up in the emotional whirlwind. Remember, your wedding dress is more than just a purchase; it's a reflection of you and the beginning of a beautiful journey. Embrace the process, trust your instincts, and find a dress that truly represents you.

Find your inspiration at damelebridal.com.

Kristin Sullivan

Founder and Creator of The Bridal Retreat

https://www.facebook.com/share/GKkfF561iSJdbdtV/?mibextid=LQQJ4d
https://www.instagram.com/thebridalretreat/
https://www.thevirtualbridalretreat.com/
https://wedoweddingplanning.etsy.com/

"Kristin Sullivan is the founder of "The Bridal Retreat" a space where wedding planning marries wellness. Her strategic, creative mind paired with her calming presence on an event day is what makes Kristin shine. Led from a place of deep service, a spirit of kindness, and master of organizational skills—Kristin has orchestrated creative weddings and one-of-a-kind events across the globe for clients over the past two decades.

No matter the celebration, be it a wedding, VIP corporate event, social celebrations, or fundraisers, Kristin delights herself in infusing her client's personalities into the details so that no two events ever look or feel alike.

Kristin holds the immense honor of being named the "Mentor for North America & The Caribbean for The Global Wedding Academy."

She takes great pride in introducing and guiding new wedding planners into the industry worldwide. She is a certified "Dare to Declare" Vision Board Instructor. She produced a wedding which aired on ABC Primetime and has been quoted in People Magazine amongst numerous other industry publications.

In addition to designing luxury celebrations, Kristin has expanded into the world of lifestyle and brand collaborations. Her mission? To help fans and fellow event planners as they create memorable events. This ambition has led her to produce several products including: Three best-selling books, a wedding journal & planning guide—SoUs: A Keepsake Book and Planner, the IDOIN30 card deck which counts down the final 30 days to wedding day, and a wedding day emergency bag HipBetty. Kristin's desire to help people celebrate all over the world leads her to continue to expand her offerings and find new outlets for her creativity.

In her spare time, Kristin loves spending time with her fur baby, her Portuguese Water Dog, Abaco. Together with Abaco, she launched The Stinky Pet Co., a luxurious, pet-friendly home fragrance product line which gives back to help fight small animal abuse & neglect. She continues her passion for writing while chasing sunsets around the globe!

To connect with Kristin, visit: www.thebridalretreat.com

Wedding Planning Marries Wellness

By Kristin Sullivan

You are about to embark on the journey of creating one of the most important days and events in your life—your wedding. Let's take a moment to recognize how that makes you feel. What is your response? Did your heart flutter a little? Did you feel your palms begin to sweat? Do you wonder where to even begin? You are not alone.

In the excitement of starting a new life with someone you cherish, the daunting task of planning a wedding also rises to the surface. Yet, this is meant to be a special time for you and those you invite into the process, such as your closest friends or family. To keep calm over the next few months, you are going to need a guide.

And that is why I want to share the best of what I have learned in two decades as a destination wedding and event planner with you. Let me sit beside you for a moment and be on your team. Together, we can kick start this season while keeping the joy in the middle of it.

Welcome to an inside peek at The Bridal Retreat, the original holistic planning experience for newly engaged Brides-to-Be. It is a sacred space of like-minded souls gathering to find guidance and support.

#1 – It Is Okay for This to Be About You

As women, we tend to shy away from being center stage. No one wants to be perceived as a bridezilla. And yet, when it comes to your wellness and your sense of peace over the next few months, let me fill you in on a little secret: It is actually *about you*.

The more you enjoy the process, elevate your wellness, and prioritize your health over the next few months—I firmly believe it impacts your sense of connection with your partner and gives your marriage a strong first year.

That is why I am such a huge advocate for wellness throughout the journey rather than once the flurry of activity is over.

In all of the thank you notes, journals, and memories I have collected over the years that I have received from my brides, do you know what I frequently hear?

I wish I would have listened to you and savored every moment.

We blinked, and it was over.

I want all of my brides to feel as if they can soak up every single moment that they want to cherish for years to come. In order to do that, a bride must feel rested, refreshed, and ready to enjoy—versus feeling drained, exhausted, and waiting for it to be over.

The key ingredient is wellness. And to achieve that, it takes you to make this season about you, prioritizing what you need over the next few months.

Let me be the first to say it: You are allowed to take care of yourself. Your wellness matters, and I am rooting for you to find it. Dare to say no to any of the wellness thieves who want to sap the joy of this moment from you.

#2 – Don't Recreate the Wheel

My biggest tip? Be unique in wedding planning elements that reflect your relationship with your partner, but for everything else, use templates.

In order to do that, I highly suggest that you consult the experts in a few top areas. Their decades of expertise mean you do not have to reinvent the wheel.

The top suggestions I recommend include:

- Wedding Planning 101: Expert crafted templates on budgeting, timelines, and vendor selection such as floral, catering, venue, music, photography, and more.

- Mindfulness and Meditation: Find a single source for your wellness. Make sure they have techniques to reduce stress and stay grounded during the busy planning phase.

- Self-Care Sessions: Stay connected to a community that is focused on maintaining a healthy lifestyle leading up to the big day.

#3 – Elevate Wellness

Wellness does not equal dieting. While many become body-conscious and focus on crash diets—this is not wellness. Instead, placing attention on what you need to feel at your peak, along with how to uplevel your energy during a demanding season, is the goal.

For all my brides, I rally around them to promote their own sense of wellness beyond the gym. Some of my favorite wellness activities to recommend include:

- Yoga and Stretching Guidance: Morning sessions to energize and center participants.

- Nature Walks and Hikes: Opportunities to connect with nature and relieve stress.

- Spa Treatments: Massages, facials, and other pampering services to help you relax.

You know what rejuvenates you. Be sure to place not only tasks on your calendar, but also time to recalibrate and restore anything that stress is seeking to snatch from you.

#4 – Seek Networking Opportunities

The wedding planning process is not a short one—and finding others who are traveling the same road can create a sense of community and belonging that helps to provide a system of support. To share stories, laughter, and advice in a cozy safe setting is a win. There are groups for this online, and in person. Anywhere that you can meet other brides and share experiences, tips, and support each other in a collaborative environment is a great addition to your journey.

Additionally, if you can attend a wedding planning showcase or local conference, you will be able to meet expert wedding vendors in a relaxed setting. This will make it easier to find the perfect fit for your special day—and partner with those you know, like, and trust.

* * *

Because I find it a joy to help strategize and dream with a bride about what her perfect day is going to look like, I have fashioned retreat experiences that are done both in person and online in order for that experience to occur.

These experiences, which are held both in person and online, place each of these elements into one place, making it a single source of reference for busy brides.

After two decades as a destination wedding and event planner, I recognized the need for a more holistic, single-stop approach to the wedding planning process. My hands-on experience revealed the need to provide brides with a space to relax, reflect, and rejuvenate while also addressing the practical aspects of planning their weddings.

Together, we cultivate a sense of calm and clarity, allowing brides to enjoy the journey leading up to their special day. This innovative approach not only enhances the planning experience but also fosters a supportive community among attendees, creating lasting connections and memories.

In order to make this experience accessible to as many brides as possible, I launched The Virtual Bridal Retreat in the summer of 2024. This allows me to provide a cost-effective solution in a virtual environment, ensuring that brides have access to time-tested templates, a range of experts in the field who are sharing their best, and a step-by-step process to work through a host of details on one smooth, seamless platform—all from the convenience of your device.

Remember to "SAY YES TO NO STRESS" and to ENJOY YOUR JOURNEY!

Cheers to Happy & Healthy Wedding Planning.

XOXO,
Kristin
www.TheVirtualBridalRetreat.com

Heather Arra

Owner of Girasole & Co. Weddings
Principal Planner

https://www.facebook.com/girasoleco
https://www.instagram.com/girasoleweddings
https://girasoleco.com/

Girasole & Co. Weddings, located in Columbus, OH, is a leading wedding planning firm that seamlessly blends artistry and elegance to craft unforgettable experiences. With nearly a decade of expertise, we specialize in designing bespoke events that authentically reflect each couple's unique love story.

Heather Arra, the owner, moved from New Jersey to Ohio with her husband in 2022 and now designs stunning spaces for couples deeply in love. Outside of work, Heather enjoys unwinding with her dog, Sadie, and binge-watching Sweet Magnolias and Virgin River.

At Girasole & Co. Weddings, we recognize the challenges of balancing wedding planning with everyday life. Our client-centered approach ensures every detail is managed with positivity, grace, and a commitment to your well-being. Our mission is to simplify the planning process and bring your vision to life. With our meticulous attention to detail and Type A personalities, we are devoted to supporting you every step of the way.

Do the *Dang Thing* That Makes You Happy

By Heather Arra

How Girasole & Co. Puts You First in Your Wedding Journey

As both a 2023 bride *and* a wedding planner, I can tell you firsthand—wedding planning can be a wild ride. There are magical moments when everything feels perfect. Then, there are times when you're on the verge of losing it. It could be over something as small as linen colors *(been there)*. The truth is, planning your dream wedding can bring out the best and worst of your emotions. If you're not careful, the stress can overshadow the joy of the journey.

Through my own experience, I learned one essential truth: your wedding should be a celebration of what makes *you* happy. Whether that's bold, colorful flowers instead of traditional whites, or trading a wedding cake for a donut wall, the goal is for your wedding to reflect who you are—not just what others expect.

At Girasole & Co. Weddings, we embrace this philosophy. While we have checklists to guide us, we don't follow a formula—we're here to create a wedding that's 100% you. We take pride in our client-focused approach and are committed to supporting your mental and emotional well-being every step of the way.

Our Client-Focused Approach: Your Wedding, Your Way

Let me tell you why Girasole & Co. is different. We're not about cookie-cutter wedding plans or one-size-fits-all approaches. Every couple is unique, and your wedding should show that. From the moment we start working together, it's all about *you*—your vision, your priorities, and your happiness. We'll listen to what makes your heart race with excitement and what keeps you up at night stressing. Then, we create a plan that brings your dream to life without you feeling overwhelmed.

At the end of the day, our job isn't just to plan a beautiful event. It's to make sure you feel supported, seen, and celebrated every step of the way. We want you to wake up on your wedding day feeling like everything is falling into place.

* * *

Honor Your Non-Negotiables

What are the moments, traditions, or details that define your love story? Whether it's a song that has special meaning, a venue that speaks to your story, or a family heirloom that needs a place of honor, identifying your "must-haves" is key. These elements will anchor your day and ensure your wedding feels deeply personal and uniquely yours.

Break Some Rules!

Traditions are great—but only if they resonate with you and your partner. Want to skip the bouquet toss and replace it with something more meaningful to you? Go for it. Dreaming of a taco truck instead of a formal sit-down dinner? Let's make it happen with flair. Your wedding is a canvas for your creativity, so break the rules and make the day unapologetically yours.

Find Your People

You need a vendor team who not only gets your vision but can also navigate the unique dynamics of your day with ease and grace. From capturing your style to managing those tricky family interactions, the right team makes all the difference. I'll guide you in finding vendors who align with your values and ensure your day is as seamless as it is magical.

Let Joy Lead the Way

When the planning process feels like too much, take a deep breath and remember why you're celebrating. Let go of the pressure for perfection and focus on what makes you happy. Your wedding is about love, laughter, and joy—not just checking off boxes. Let your instincts lead, and together we'll create a day full of meaningful moments that truly shine.

* * *

Seeing Is Believing: Visualizing Your Dream Wedding

Ever get stuck imagining what your big day will *actually* look like? You've pinned a million inspiration boards, but somehow the vision still feels fuzzy. That's where we come in. With tools like Aisle Planner and Canva, we create mock-ups of your ceremony and reception, down to seating arrangements and floral displays. Being able to *see* your wedding helps you make confident choices, making the whole process smoother.

The Mental Health Factor: We Get It

Wedding planning can be intense. As someone who has felt the weight of those tiny details, I know how it feels, and that's why mental health support is part of our mission. We break down the process into manageable steps, so you never feel overwhelmed. A portion of every wedding we plan goes to mental health organizations because we believe in supporting not just our clients, but our community as well.

Do What Makes You Happy

Here's my biggest piece of advice: do what makes *you* happy. It's your wedding day, and it should reflect your love story. Don't get bogged down by trends, family opinions, or what Pinterest says is "perfect." If you've always wanted a sunset ceremony on a mountaintop—let's do it.

If a cocktail hour by the beach is your vision—let's bring it to life. If you'd rather exchange vows under a canopy of twinkling lights instead of in a traditional venue—let's make that magic happen. And if you want to shimmy down the aisle instead of walking—let's turn up the music and dance!

At Girasole & Co., we empower you to make choices that feel right for you. Whether it's a glamorous ballroom wedding or an intimate backyard celebration, we bring your vision to life. We'll be your biggest cheerleaders, celebrating each win, helping through challenges, and making sure your day is perfect.

Your Midwest Wedding Planning BFF

Here's the thing—wedding planning might feel overwhelming at times, but it should also be an exciting adventure! When you work with us, you're not just hiring a planner; you're gaining a team that's just as excited about your big day as you are. We turn the chaos into manageable steps, and bring your vision to life seamlessly. Think of us as your wedding planning BFFs—ready to support you whenever it feels like too much and just as thrilled as you when everything comes together perfectly.

Why Girasole & Co. Weddings?

1. **Client-Focused Planning**: Your wedding should be a reflection of *you*, and that's why our approach is entirely client-focused. We listen to your needs, respect your boundaries, and build a planning process around your comfort and happiness.

2. **Visualization Tools**: We take your ideas and make them tangible with mock-ups on Aisle Planner and Canva. You'll see every detail come to life before the big day, allowing you to make confident decisions.

3. **Mental Health Support**: Wedding planning can be emotionally draining. We prioritize your mental well-being. We also donate to mental health organizations to support the cause.

4. **Your Personal Cheerleaders**: We're not just your planners, we're your partners in this journey. We'll celebrate your highs, support you through the lows, and ensure that your wedding day is everything you've ever wanted.

Let's Do the Dang Thing—Together

At Girasole & Co., we're here to help you do the dang thing that makes you happy. You may be dreaming of a glamorous ballroom wedding. Or perhaps an intimate backyard celebration is more your style. We'll bring your vision to life in a way that reflects your unique style and personality.

Let's chat about making your wedding planning experience joyful, stress-free, and completely *yours*. After all, it's your day—and we're thrilled to help you make it unforgettable.

Always here for you,
Heather Arra
www.girasoleco.com

Callie Rackley Carr

Founder of CALLIE CARR EVENTS

https://www.facebook.com/calliecarrevents
https://www.instagram.com/calliecarrevents/
https://calliecarrevents.com/

Callie Rackley Carr is a distinguished Accredited Wedding Planner based in Warner Robins, Georgia, renowned for her exceptional skills in orchestrating memorable events across the Southeast. She rebranded her company from Sister Secrets Wedding & Event Planning to its current identity in 2021, Callie Carr Events, having planned events since 2012. Callie's expertise and commitment to her craft are evident through her active involvement in the Association of Bridal Consultants, where she serves as Georgia State Manager. Her journey into wedding planning was preceded by a solid educational foundation and diverse professional experiences. Callie earned her Associate Degree in Human Services from Abraham Baldwin Agricultural College before obtaining her Wedding Planner Certificate from Penn Foster College. She furthered her education with a Bachelor's of Science in Psychology, complemented by a Minor in Sociology, from Troy University.

Hire A High Energy Hype Queen: The Wedding Planning Process Explained

By Callie Rackley Carr

Planning a wedding can be one of the most exciting yet overwhelming experiences in a couple's life. With so many decisions to be made, tasks to be completed, and details to iron out, it's easy to feel a bit lost in the process. This is where a high-energy wedding planner comes in, even if you are not high-energy yourself. A fun wedding planner isn't just about organizing logistics; they specialize in creating a fun, stress-free, and memorable experience for the couple and their guests.

The role of a wedding planner has evolved over time, and today, it's about much more than checking off boxes on a to-do list. You want someone who brings joy, energy, and creativity to every aspect of the wedding process. Whether it's choosing the perfect venue, designing unique décor, or handling the nitty-gritty details, a high-energy wedding planner ensures that the wedding planning journey is as enjoyable as the big day itself.

I can tell you that choosing a wedding planner with expertise can be the biggest decision for your Wedding Day. One of the best compliments I have ever received at a wedding was from the grandfather of the bride. He said… "You have the most beautiful smile, and you can tell you really love what you do." How powerful is that? This is after he sees me emptying trash cans, bringing the couple a snack plate and drink, moving tables and centerpieces to repurpose them from the ceremony to the reception, and checking in with all the vendors to make sure they have what they need. As a planner, I am constantly moving on the Wedding Day, I do not eat until everyone in the building has, my feet are throbbing, and sometimes sweating (haha), but you never know what guests are noticing about you. This is exactly what I want people to see when they hire me for their event. You want someone who exudes joy and excitement because this is one of the most important days of the couple's life.

You may think your aunt or cousin who has planned a birthday party can handle the task, but what happens if it gets to the Wedding Day and they cannot? Let me tell you what to look for in a Wedding Planner...

- High Energy (this is your hype person to pump you up about everything YOU). Nothing is worse than getting excited about something and telling your fiancé/friend/family member that they do not meet your energy. Sigh. You want someone who is going to be every bit as excited as you are about every detail and creating the vision that you want within your means of doing it.

- Problem Solver – If the cake collapses or the cake topper breaks, who will be the one to fix it? What happens if a guest has a food allergy you were not aware of and needs to find out what they can eat? Making sure the wedding party doesn't overdrink during the wedding day and has food in their bellies until dinner is served. Having someone who can navigate any problem throughout the night without having to come to you every 5 minutes and worry you with questions. We may laugh about it later, but at the moment, it is handled.

- Attention to Detail – You paid good money for your photography/videography, and I want to make sure you get the shots you envisioned. From straightening the chairs, clearing the room of any guests so that you can get a full room photo, gathering your details together so you can have those memorable items photographed, raining outside? A clear umbrella shot is a must, and THIS wedding planner keeps it in their emergency kit. Your wedding planner will work very closely with your photographer/videographer throughout the event to make sure those memories are captured.

- Communication and Creativity – You want to be heard and validated!! Clear communication between your wedding planners is a must, they are your advocate to make sure that your needs/wants are executed. Having creative talent is essential as well, to make sure that every little detail is thought about, from the guestbook table to the table settings.

* * *

WHAT TO EXPECT

A wedding planner's services often begin with an initial consultation where they learn about the couple's vision, preferences, personalities, and wedding day goals. This is the perfect opportunity for the couple to get to know their planner and see if their styles align. The planner will ask thoughtful questions to uncover details about the couple's personality. A wedding planner aims to make the wedding feel authentic to the couple. They'll explore things like favorite colors, activities, hobbies, and even the couple's love story to incorporate meaningful elements into the wedding.

FUN MEMORY: *A previous couple happened to be golf pros and wanted to add that unique touch to the Wedding Day somehow. The venue was located at the golf course where the bride was currently employed, and they set up a putting green for guests to participate in during the cocktail hour.*

$$$: While the planner's role is to bring the couple's dream wedding to life, they will also guide them to stay within their budget, offering creative alternatives when necessary. There are normally a few areas of the planning process that the couple feels are more important, for example, it may be food and music or floral and photography. Those areas are going to have more of the budget applied. It is helpful for the couple to understand the generalized costs of different areas of the wedding booking process so they can plan accordingly.

Theme & Vision: Whether it's a glamorous black-tie affair or a relaxed beach ceremony, the planner will help create a cohesive theme or concept that fits the couple's style. They might offer unique suggestions that reflect the couple's shared interests or their story.

FUN MEMORY: A couple wanted all the guests to wear black and had the vision of a sleek photo of perfectly dressed guests. No matter how specific on the invite, there were still a few guests who thought it was optional and arrived wearing a gold top or pink dress in a sea of black-on-black attire. Don't worry, Aunt Judy was allowed to stay, and many laughs were had.

Creative Vision: A wedding planner can help bring your vision to life, offering creative ideas that you might not have thought of. They know how to transform a venue and incorporate your personal style into every detail, from the decorations to the flow of the ceremony. I always like to remind clients to add a personal touch to the vision. This is, after all, a day to celebrate your love. Examples could include photos of your pets on koozies or napkins, one of the cakes showing your favorite sports team, incorporating how you met, or hobbies you enjoy. Your guests will love to see this throughout the floor plan to remind them of how amazing you both are.

FUN MEMORY: The couple was an avid Star Wars fan and bought colored light sabers to use for the grand exit. Guests were able to take these home as a favor.

Expertise and Experience: Wedding planners are experts in coordinating all aspects of a wedding, from the timeline to the budget. Their experience helps navigate potential issues and knock them out before they become problems. They are also well-versed in current trends, vendor recommendations, and logistical best practices. When you make the decision to choose a Wedding Planner, ask about how many years they have been doing this, what a typical day looks like (logistic-wise), and what problems they have solved on the Wedding

Day to execute the client's wishes. These questions will help vet your choice.

FUN MEMORY: *If not doing an assigned seating chart, reserved tables are normally noted nearest the dance floor for the immediate family. Many times, the tables have been labeled reserved for "family" and the bride and groom's 2nd and 3rd cousins fill those seats, leaving the mother/father of the couple without a seat. This is something I can monitor and make sure doesn't happen. While you are taking photos, your VIP family members do not have to worry about where they will be seated for the reception.*

Stress Reduction: Who wants to stress about why the cake hasn't arrived or making sure the chairs are perfectly spaced while you are trying to be pampered with hair and makeup? Weddings have many moving parts to manage. A wedding planner takes on the heavy lifting—handling contracts, making sure timelines are followed, and troubleshooting any problems that arise. This allows you to enjoy the process rather than getting overwhelmed by the details. Even for the couple who wants to take charge of all of the planning process up until the Wedding Day, being able to hand that responsibility off (knowing your wishes will be fulfilled) lifts that weight off your shoulders.

FUN MEMORY: *A previous bride had a sacred Wedding Planning binder that she used throughout the wedding planning process. On rehearsal day, it was left on the back of her stepfather's truck and when he drove off, the papers went flying in a paper tornado effect on the road. They were able to go back and pick up the pieces, but rest assured, even without the binder... I had all the details, and couple's wishes in place on Wedding Day.*

Vendor Selection and Management: A great wedding is made up of more than just a beautiful venue and décor—it's about the people who bring it all to life. A wedding planner has an extensive network of trusted vendors, and part of their job is recommending and managing these professionals. The vendor selection process can be daunting, but a skilled planner knows the best options for every aspect of the wedding.

Catering: A wedding planner will work closely with caterers to ensure the food and drink menu aligns with the couple's tastes and dietary requirements. They'll also help with food presentation, choosing the right style of service (plated, buffet, family-style), and handling any logistics around the meal. Answering questions such as, is this too much food? Should we do a cocktail hour menu? Is a champagne toast necessary? Should you provide the plates/cutlery, or will the caterer provide this? Will the caterer cut the cake for my guests?

Photography and Videography: Capturing the magic of the wedding day is essential, and a wedding planner will connect the couple with photographers and videographers who have experience in creating beautiful, candid moments that reflect the wedding's vibe. Every photographer has a different style of editing and shooting, it is a detail that the couple must choose from to match their ideal vision. Do you want laid-back and candid shots? Moody tones or light and airy editing style?

Floral Design: Flowers add romance and beauty to the wedding day, and the planner will help select the perfect floral designer to bring the couple's dreams to life. What is the difference between a florist and a floral designer? A florist may create a centerpiece and drop it off for you to display, specializing in pickup and delivery services for birthdays/funerals/anniversaries. A floral designer is going to make sure all of the décor pieces align with the central theme, bring additional design elements to tie the table together, on-site installation of décor, and break down at the end of the night.

Entertainment: A wedding planner knows that entertainment is key to creating a lively atmosphere. They'll recommend bands, DJs, or performers who will keep the party going all night long. From personalized playlists to interactive games, the entertainment adds energy to the event.

Hair and Makeup Artists: A wedding planner will know exactly who to call for flawless bridal hair and makeup. They ensure that the bride and bridal party are treated to an enjoyable experience, making everyone feel pampered and beautiful on the big day.

Timeline and Day of Coordination: A wedding day is a carefully orchestrated event, and a wedding planner takes care of every timing detail to ensure it runs smoothly. From the moment the couple wakes up to the last song of the evening, a wedding planner handles the entire schedule so the couple can relax and enjoy the day. The couple is released following rehearsal and hands over the "official" reigns to the wedding planner to execute.

Creating a Wedding Day Timeline: The planner works with all vendors and the couple to create a detailed timeline that ensures everything happens on time. This includes everything from hair and makeup schedules to when guests should arrive, when dinner will be served, and when the first dance will happen.

Coordinating with Vendors: On the wedding day, the planner acts as the main point of contact for all vendors, making sure each one arrives on time, sets up properly, and follows through with their responsibilities.

Guest Management: Ensuring that guests are welcomed and guided through the event is also a key responsibility. The planner makes sure guests are seated at the ceremony, directs them to cocktail hour, and ensures everything flows seamlessly throughout the evening.

Problem Solving: No matter how well you plan, things can go wrong on the big day. Whether it's bad weather, a vendor running late, or a sudden change in plans, a wedding planner is there to troubleshoot and solve problems without you even knowing. Their experience ensures that any mishap is handled quickly and professionally. This may be one of the most important areas of the Wedding Day. So many things can and could go sideways on the Wedding Day, and knowing how to efficiently navigate the problem when it arises (without alarming the couple) is essential. Not only is your Wedding Planner serving you on the Wedding Day but serving your beloved friends and family.

Managing the Ceremony: The planner ensures that the ceremony starts on time, with everyone in the right place. Making sure all cell phones are off, no one has gum in their mouth, bouquets are held at the waist, and dress and jewelry are in place. This includes coordinating the bridal party's entrance, managing the music cues, and ensuring the couple is in the spotlight.

Reception Coordination: At the reception, the wedding planner makes sure the couple enjoys the celebration by handling logistics behind the scenes. They'll help with the grand entrance, speeches, cutting the cake, and any special traditions or surprises the couple has planned.

Post-Wedding Services: Once the wedding is over, a wedding planner continues to provide support to ensure everything wraps up smoothly and that the couple's memories are well-preserved, gathering all your personal items for load out. Your wedding planner should be there throughout the entire event and make sure all guests and the couple depart from the venue. Peace of Mind... Is Priceless!!

When you think back on your wedding day (which EVERYONE does), you do not want to remember how stressed you were and how you wish things could have been handled differently. A wedding planner does not give you a physical, tangible item when you hire them for your Wedding, sometimes that is hard for couples to understand. A floral designer gives you beautiful flowers, caterers give you yummy food, a photographer/videographer gives you memorable photographs and videography to cherish for years, the DJ/Band gives you the vibe for the dance floor, hair and makeup give you that polished rock star look for all to admire. What does a Wedding Planner give you? Let me drop a few nuggets for you to consider. Imagine you are getting married, and the day of panic starts to set in...

- I forgot a cake cutter and don't want to use a plastic knife for the official cake cutting photos!!

- My toasting glasses don't have any champagne poured and it's time for speeches!!

- You are at the altar for rehearsal and don't know what to do with your hands, how does the hand off take place? Where do I stand?

- You enter the reception, that neon sign you spent so much money on, who turns that on? Did the photographer get a photo of it?

- I brought glow sticks for the dance floor, who takes the wrappers and little tags off of EVERY single glow stick?

- The guys are ready for photos, but they have the grandmother's flowers pinned on instead of the groomsmen boutonnieres.

- I booked a photobooth, but I don't think I ever got a chance to get in it.

- Where do my grandparents sit at the ceremony? My best side is my right side, can I stand on the opposite side at the altar?

- Who lights the candles? Collects my gift cards and gifts? Boxes up my left-over cake? Preserves my bouquet so I can take it home? Makes sure the marriage license is signed by the officiant?

- When is sunset? I would love to get sunset photos? Where are the best photo locations at my venue?

- What happens if someone comes late to the ceremony? I want a private moment with my husband right after the ceremony, how do I keep guests away?

- The unity candle doesn't have a lighter!!

- I am about to walk down the aisle; I am so thirsty!! I need a sip of water...

- Time for entering the reception, how do I bustle this dress? Where do we go when we walk in? I don't want to dance the entire song; how can we shorten things up?

- Time for the sparkler exit, oh wait... where do the sparklers go after we are done? I didn't bring a bucket for that!!

Hire that High Energy Hype Queen of a Wedding Planner!! Your Wedding Planner becomes a gift to yourself, to be as stress free as possible!! Happy Planning!!

Jean Neuhart

Weddings From The Heart
Wedding Specialist

https://www.linkedin.com/in/jeanneuhart
https://www.facebook.com/wedbyjean
https://www.instagram.com/wedbyjean/
https://weddingsfromtheheartblog.net/

Jean Neuhart is a sought-after wedding expert with 30 years of industry experience. Known for her no-nonsense, practical advice, her insights have been featured in The Knot, Newsweek, and Good Housekeeping, as well as on local television and popular wedding podcasts. Jean is also the author of two wedding planning books: Wedding Invitations, RSVPs, and More! Oh My! and From 'I Will' to 'I Do', which provide invaluable guidance for couples navigating their wedding journey.

While Jean no longer coordinates weddings, she continues to guide couples through the planning process with 1:1 online consultations, digital tools, and her blog, Weddings From The Heart. Her blog offers creative, stress-free advice to help couples plan meaningful, personalized celebrations.

Jean is passionate about helping couples create meaningful, personalized weddings. When not offering wedding wisdom, Jean enjoys reading horror novels and spending time with her family dog.

Visit her at weddingsfromtheheartblog.net

Why Experience Matters: The Essential Role of Professional Vendors in Your Wedding

By Jean Neuhart

Your wedding day is not just any other party; it is a celebration of your love, commitment, and hopes for the future. Not only is it the culmination of hopes and dreams, not to mention months (or even years) of planning, it is also the culmination of significant investments: the emotional investment in creating a day that is meaningful, memorable, and reflective of your personal love story; and the financial investment, often involving substantial savings or even loans, to bring that vision to life.

Every detail contributes to the overall experience. So, with all of this at stake, ensuring that every detail is flawlessly executed becomes paramount, making the choice of experienced, professional vendors essential to achieving the perfect day (well, at least one that is as perfect as humanly possible). From the planner who brings your vision to life, to the photographer who captures every precious moment, and the caterer who ensures your guests are well-fed and happy, and so on, each vendor plays a pivotal role in creating a seamless, stress-free, memorable experience. The success of your wedding day rests on the collective efforts of the team behind the scenes, and this is where experience comes into play.

The expertise and reliability of your vendors can mean the difference between a wedding day that runs smoothly and just how you planned, and one fraught with stress, confusion, and unexpected challenges and mishaps. In this chapter, we will explore the crucial impact that experienced vendors have on your wedding day, and why investing in their expertise is one of the best decisions you can make.

Real-Life Story (Short Version)

Just a few months before the wedding, I received a frantic call from the bride's mother. Her sister, who had taken on the role of planner, had promised to handle the caterer, bartenders, rentals, and band—but everything was unraveling. The caterer, bartenders, and rentals had fallen through, and soon after, the band demanded double the agreed-upon price and additional perks. And that was just the beginning. There were many other issues at play, but to keep it brief, I stepped in and not only was able to secure reliable new vendors, but found the perfect caterer, rentals, bartenders, band, florist, and even a videographer—rescuing the wedding and ensuring a beautiful, seamless day.

What Defines a Professional Vendor?

As we've determined above, your wedding vendor team plays a crucial role in ensuring your wedding runs smoothly and that your expectations are met. Hiring professional wedding vendors is the best way to ensure that happens. However, a professional wedding vendor is defined by more than just their ability to provide a service. So, how to recognize a "professional" among the sea of wedding vendors out there? Here are 5 key areas to look into:

Industry Experience and Skill

A professional vendor will have a wealth of experience, specialized training and education, and refined skills in their specific area of expertise, such as catering, photography, or floral design. This experience, etc., allows them to consistently deliver high-quality services/products.

Clear Contracts and Communication

Professionals provide detailed contracts that clearly outline their services, pricing, deadlines, and expectations. They maintain clear, timely communication with the couple and other vendors, providing updates, answering questions, and addressing concerns promptly to avoid any misunderstandings and to ensure everyone is on the same page.

Meeting Deadlines/Reliability and Consistency

Professional vendors are responsible for adhering to set deadlines, such as delivering a product (like wedding invitations), following through on commitments (like completing setup on the wedding day itself), and maintaining high standards, ensuring that the entire wedding process from planning to the wedding day itself goes smoothly. Couples can confidently rely on them to show up on time and deliver what was promised.

Adapting to Changes/Problem-Solving Skills

Wedding plans can change for various reasons, from the couple making a change in plans to an unexpected forecast of rain on the wedding day. Professional vendors need to be flexible and adapt to any last-minute changes while staying calm and professional, no matter what comes up.

Legal Compliance and Ethical Practices

Vendors must ensure they meet all legal requirements, and have proper licenses and insurance in place. They should provide a contract or letter of agreement that clearly defines their terms, payment schedules, and responsibilities. They operate with integrity, ensuring transparency, fairness, and respect for the couple and other vendors involved, and maintain a strong reputation within the wedding industry/community.

To sum up, professional vendors bring a wealth of knowledge and expertise to your wedding planning process. Their experience enables them to deliver services with precision and confidence. Simply put, they know what works, what doesn't, and how to achieve your desired outcome. This allows them to offer invaluable insights and suggestions that can elevate and refine your wedding vision.

Key Vendor Roles and Their Impact

A wedding is much like an orchestra, with each vendor serving as a distinct instrument. When experienced professionals are at the helm, these instruments come together in perfect harmony, creating a beautiful symphony. However, if one or more vendors lack experience or approach their role as a mere hobby, the result can be a discordant performance. The following describes the key vendors and illustrates how each contributes to the overall success of your wedding.

The Wedding Planner

A wedding planner wears many hats—architect of the day, team leader, and conductor of the 'orchestra.' Their role is to help you define your vision, set everything in motion, and on the wedding day, execute the plan so all elements come together seamlessly. Their expertise spans wedding history, modern alternatives, and etiquette, ensuring everything aligns with your values and preferences. From creating planning checklists to troubleshooting behind the scenes, they navigate logistics and provide emotional support during stressful moments. A skilled wedding planner is the key to a stress-free, beautifully executed celebration.

The Photographer/Videographer

Your photographer and videographer play essential roles in capturing the special moments of your wedding day, turning them into lasting memories and cherished family heirlooms. While anyone can 'point and shoot,' a professional goes beyond simply documenting events. They are storytellers who expertly capture the essence of your day. With a keen eye for candid moments, emotional exchanges, and unique details, experienced professionals anticipate key moments—ensuring nothing is missed, including The Kiss (there are no do-overs). Their technical skills also allow them to handle challenging lighting (such as the popular sunset photos), unpredictable weather, and tight schedules effortlessly. The images and footage they create will become treasured keepsakes, allowing you and future generations to relive your wedding day's magic for years to come.

The Caterer

Food is often a highlight of any wedding celebration, and your caterer is responsible for creating a memorable dining experience. Their role goes beyond preparing delicious dishes. An experienced caterer expertly manages timing, presentation, and flavor to ensure each dish is served at its best. They accommodate special dietary needs with flavorful options and understand that their job extends beyond the kitchen. From elegant table settings to attentive staff who serve, replenish, and clean up, a skilled caterer leaves your guests not only well-fed but impressed, enhancing the overall success of your celebration.

The Florist

One of the best ways to express your wedding vision is through your décor, with flowers being the most popular choice. Creating stunning arrangements involves more than just placing flowers in a vase—it requires skill and attention to detail to keep them looking fresh all day. This is where a professional florist shines. They know which blooms are in season, which types are hardy enough to last all day, how to prep each stem, and how to select flowers that will be at their peak during your event. They know how to handle delicate blooms to prevent wilting or browning and expertly manage the logistics of transporting, delivering, and setting up the arrangements on time.

The Entertainment/DJ

No party is complete without entertainment, and a live band or DJ sets the tone for the evening, keeping the energy and mood high. A Spotify playlist won't cut it. A professional DJ does more than just 'press play'—they read the crowd, knowing exactly when to switch up songs to keep guests engaged and the dance floor lively. They seamlessly transition between tracks, avoiding any awkward silences. As the evening's MC, they're skilled at making timely announcements and ensuring the event flows smoothly. Plus, a professional always comes prepared with backup equipment to handle any unforeseen technical issues.

Real-Life Story

Before giving the album to the newlyweds, the photographer let me take a peek. One photo showed the hood and grill of their getaway car in the church parking lot (a 1940-something Cadillac convertible borrowed from the bride's uncle). I thought, 'Okay, a picture of the car, but...?' Then the photographer pointed to the hood. Reflected perfectly on the glossy surface was the couple, sharing a spontaneous kiss. On the opposite page was another shot of them standing next to the car, as the groom dipped the bride for another playful kiss. Both were unique, unplanned moments—no do-overs. An inexperienced photographer might have missed them, but with over 20 years in the business, this one knew exactly how to capture those fleeting, magical moments.

Common Risks/Issues with Inexperienced Vendors

It's easy to see why couples might consider hiring less experienced vendors—perhaps they're more affordable, or you want to support someone new in the business. While saving money is important and helping someone get their start is admirable, is your wedding day—a once-in-a-lifetime event—the right time to take those risks?

Hiring inexperienced vendors can expose your wedding day to significant pitfalls, turning what should be a seamless celebration into a day full of stress and disappointment.

Planner/Coordinator

- Struggles with organization, unable to juggle the many moving parts of the day. A wedding has so many intricate details, and if they can't keep things on track, chaos can follow.
- Poor logistical skills mean timing issues and disruptions. Imagine your cake arriving late or your ceremony starting without key guests because no one was in charge.
- They might over-promise and under-deliver, leaving you with unmet expectations when it's too late to fix things.

Photographer

- Lack of professional equipment—or worse, no backup—can result in blurry photos, missed moments, or a total technical failure.
- Inexperienced photographers can miss irreplaceable shots like the first kiss, the emotional first look, or the grand entrance, all because they don't know where to be or when to capture that fleeting moment.
- Inefficiency in managing time could cause delays, meaning less time for portraits or rushing through key parts of the day, leaving you stressed and flustered.

Caterer

- Not providing enough food or poorly prepared dishes can leave your guests hungry and unimpressed. Imagine hearing whispers of grumbling stomachs at your reception.
- If they don't bring enough staff, your guests might be left waiting too long for meals or drinks or sitting with dirty plates and glasses all evening, which can quickly sour the atmosphere.

Florist

- Choosing flowers that aren't hardy enough means you could end up with wilted or brown blooms before the reception even begins, ruining your carefully planned décor.
- Inexperienced handling of flowers could result in bruised, damaged arrangements that don't hold up to the day's demands.
- Failure to select in-season flowers could lead to costly imports or, worse, a lack of availability, forcing last-minute changes to your floral design.

DJ

- Poor sound equipment can cause audio issues, from crackling speakers to music cutting out at key moments.
- If the DJ can't read the room, your dance floor could end up empty instead of packed with guests having a great time.
- Lack of MC skills means missed cues for important events like toasts or cake cutting, leaving your guests confused and the timeline off-balance.

Real-Life Story

It's no secret that a DJ plays a crucial role in a reception's success. Being a DJ is more than just playing songs from a list—it's about controlling the momentum and balancing upbeat and slow tunes to keep guests engaged. At one reception, the dance floor was packed until the DJ switched to a slow song. The floor cleared, but instead of reading the room, he followed it with another slow tune, leaving the bride disappointed. When he started a third, I asked if he could play something more upbeat. His response was that he's playing songs from the bride's playlist. I then asked him to play something upbeat from that playlist. When he did as I asked, the guests quickly filled the dance floor again.

Problems with Relying on Friends or Family Members

Choosing a friend or family member to provide a wedding service can be tempting for many couples. There's a special, personal touch in having someone close to you play a role in your big day that no hired vendor can replicate. Perhaps your friend is launching a new photography business, or your cousin is trying their hand at DJing—hiring them feels like a win-win, giving them valuable experience while saving you money. And, of course, the reduced cost is hard to resist. But before you commit, it's important to consider the potential risks and challenges that come with this decision.

While asking friends or family members to handle wedding tasks might seem like a budget-friendly solution, it can lead to problems that could negatively impact your wedding day. Even with the best intentions, they may lack the experience needed to manage critical responsibilities. As the saying goes, 'they don't know what they don't know,' which could lead to important details being overlooked. They might also lack the technical skills or professional equipment to deliver their service properly.

The line between 'vendor' and 'guest' often blurs in these situations. Will they focus on their role or get caught up in the celebration? If they're working, they might feel left out of the festivities. But if they're partying, they're more likely to miss key moments—moments you can't get back. Choosing a friend or family member may seem like a good idea, but it's important to weigh the risks before making your decision.

Even with the best intentions, friends and family might assume that knowing you well equates to knowing what you want from their service. This assumption can lead to misunderstandings, missed expectations, and even conflict or disappointment—potentially straining or damaging your relationship. In contrast, a professional understands the value of detailed discussions and consultations, ensuring that every aspect aligns with your vision and avoiding unwelcome surprises on your big day.

Relying on a professional to fix mistakes is much easier—they have backup equipment and can compensate for errors if needed. However, with friends or family, it's trickier. They often act based on their assumptions and may lack the resources to correct mistakes. Worse, it can permanently damage your relationship or create long-term family tension.

Real-Life Story

To save money, the couple opted for family-catered food at their wedding reception. While the dishes were delicious, several issues arose that could have been avoided with professional catering. The family arrived late, leading to a rushed buffet setup. They forgot essential serving utensils, requiring someone to make a last-minute run. Some food options ran low, and improper use of rented chafing dishes resulted in scorch marks—incurring an extra fee from the rental company.

How to Identify and Choose Experienced Vendors

Not all vendors who label themselves as 'professionals' are created equally. Some are more like hobbyists—while they may have passion and talent, their approach can be casual or unrefined. On the other hand, true professionals not only possess the necessary skills but continuously hone them. They invest in their craft by attending educational seminars, staying up-to-date on industry trends, and purchasing professional-grade equipment (with backups on hand). These efforts ensure they're fully prepared to deliver the high-quality service your wedding deserves.

Like with any important decision in life, you'll want to do your research. For many engaged couples, the first question that comes to mind is,

'How much do your services cost?' Of course, budget matters, and finding someone who fits within your price range is essential. But be cautious about choosing a vendor based solely on cost. The cheapest option isn't always the best one. If a vendor's pricing is significantly lower—or higher—than others, there's usually a reason for it, and that reason can impact the quality of your wedding day.

So, how do you sift through the options and pinpoint the true professionals? Here's what to look for:

Several factors contribute to a vendor's pricing, including:

- Overhead expenses (e.g., rent, insurance, marketing)
- Labor costs (e.g., paying staff, assistants)
- Quality and type of materials or equipment

However, some factors that can directly affect your wedding include:

- Less experience or fewer qualifications
- Lack of membership in trade organizations
- Limited education or training in their field
- Time commitment (how much time they will actually dedicate to your wedding)

While budget is a crucial consideration, remember to weigh the value and quality a vendor offers. A higher price often reflects a stronger commitment to delivering a seamless and unforgettable wedding experience.

Key questions to ask your potential vendor:

- How long have you been in business?
- Do you work solo, or will you have assistants on the wedding day?
- What specific services will you provide?
- How many weddings do you typically handle in a weekend?

- Do you provide a contract? (If the answer is no, move on.)
- What is your cancellation/rescheduling policy?
- What is your price, and what does it include?
- Are there any additional fees?
- What is your policy on overtime, and how is it priced?

Beyond just asking questions, aim to have a genuine conversation with them. Trust your instincts. How the vendor makes you feel is just as important as their answers. Do they respond confidently and professionally? Do they make you feel like a priority? These impressions can be telling signs of how they'll handle your big day.

Selecting experienced vendors ensures you'll have professionals who can handle any challenges, understand your vision, and deliver quality service. With their skills and experience, you can feel confident that your big day will be beautifully executed and well-coordinated.

When searching for wedding vendors, it's important to ask about their background, experience, and training. But asking them *why* they do what they do can be even more revealing. Are they passionate about seeing all the planning come together and knowing they helped create lasting memories? Do they love photography because it allows them to tell stories, and there's no greater story than a wedding day? Or are they simply doing it on the side to make some extra money? (Yes, that was the actual reason from a vendor.) The 'why' can tell you if they're truly invested in making your day special.

The Peace of Mind Provided by Professional Vendors

You've worked hard and spent countless hours planning the wedding of your dreams, investing both time and money to make everything perfect. The last thing you want is to spend your wedding day worrying about whether the cake has arrived on time, if the centerpieces have the right flowers, or whether there's enough food for your guests. What you truly need on your special day is peace of mind—the ability to relax and fully enjoy each moment. By hiring a seasoned, professional vendor team, you can trust that every detail is in expert hands, ensuring that your day runs smoothly and stress-free.

This peace of mind allows you to fully immerse yourself and truly experience each special moment, from the emotional exchange of vows to dancing and celebrating with your loved ones. Instead of worrying about logistics, you can focus on what truly matters—cherishing every smile, every tear, and every dance move, knowing that your vision is being expertly brought to life. With experienced vendors handling the details, you're free to relax and enjoy the magic of the day.

On the other hand, choosing inexperienced vendors or relying on friends and family for essential services can inadvertently lead to added stress and uncertainty. Without having the expertise of seasoned professionals by your side, small details can slip through the cracks, errors can be made, key tasks or responsibilities can be forgotten, and the unexpected becomes harder to manage.

Instead of feeling confident that everything is running smoothly, you may find yourself worrying about whether timelines are being followed, if key moments are being captured, or if the overall quality of the day is what you envisioned. The peace of mind that should come naturally can quickly be replaced with anxiety and distraction, and possible regret after the day is over.

Ultimately, the peace of mind that comes from hiring seasoned vendors allows you to fully enjoy your wedding day without distraction. Investing in experienced vendors not only alleviates stress but also enhances your overall wedding experience. By entrusting your vision to professionals, you can fully immerse yourself in the magic of the moment.

As I mentioned at the beginning, your wedding day is not just any other party; it should be a joyful celebration filled with love, laughter, and unforgettable memories, surrounded by your loved ones—not a day spent worrying about logistics or mishaps. By investing in experienced, professional vendors, remember that you're not just paying for services; you're securing peace of mind. On this once-in-a-lifetime occasion, you deserve the best. With the right team by your side, your wedding day will be everything you've dreamed of—and more.

Beverly Little

Founder and CEO of Tying Knots & Stamping Papers, LLC

https://www.facebook.com/tyingknotsandstampingpapers/
https://www.instagram.com/tyingknots.stampingpapers/
https://tyingknotsstampingpapers.com/

Beverly Little is the CEO/Founder of Tying Knots & Stamping Papers, bringing passion and precision to every ceremony she oversees as a Notary, Minister, and Wedding Officiant. Known for her meticulous attention to detail and warm professionalism, Beverly specializes in crafting both traditional and non-traditional weddings tailored to each couple's unique story. Her expertise includes on-site ceremonies and destination weddings, making her a sought-after choice for those looking to say "I do" in meaningful and memorable locations. With a personal touch and deep commitment to her clients, Beverly ensures that each couple's wedding day reflects their personality and vision, whether they are drawn to classic elegance or modern, unique approaches. Through Tying Knots & Stamping Papers, she's not only creating ceremonies but also cherished moments that last a lifetime.

How to Choose the Right Wedding Officiant for Your Ceremony

By Beverly Little

Planning your wedding involves countless details, each adding its own touch to your special day. However, among the cake tastings, venue choices, and decor decisions, one critical aspect often deserves more attention: selecting your wedding officiant. Your officiant isn't just there to lead the ceremony; they are the voice and heart that sets the tone for the celebration of your love story. Here, we'll walk you through what to look for in an officiant and how to find the perfect person for your ceremony.

* * *

What Is a Wedding Officiant, and Why Do You Need One?

A wedding officiant is authorized to conduct a marriage ceremony and ensure that the event is legally recognized. Officiants can be religious leaders, judges, professional celebrants, or even legally ordained close friends or family members.

In essence, your officiant plays a significant role in guiding the exchange of vows, making legal pronouncements, and creating a memorable experience that reflects your love and values. Choosing the right person ensures the ceremony feels meaningful, personalized, and true to your relationship.

Benefits of Having a Wedding Officiant

A wedding officiant can bring a professional touch to your ceremony, helping ease pre-wedding jitters and create a natural and well-paced flow. Here are some key benefits:

1. **Experience and Guidance:** Experienced officiants understand how to structure a ceremony. They'll know when to add lighthearted moments, when to pause for emotional highlights, and how to make your vows stand out.

2. **Personalization:** Many officiants are skilled storytellers who craft ceremonies that reflect your unique relationship, adding anecdotes or details that make your love story shine.

3. **Legal Validity:** Your officiant is crucial in ensuring your marriage is legally binding by completing the necessary paperwork and fulfilling local requirements.

4. **Emotional Support:** Officiants often have a calming presence, helping ease nervousness with their guidance and confidence.

* * *

If You're Having a Religious Ceremony...

For couples planning a religious ceremony, an officiant is typically a representative of their faith, such as a priest, rabbi, minister, imam, or other religious leader. Choosing a religious officiant often aligns with tradition, spiritual beliefs, and family values. Still, it's essential to confirm that they can cater to your preferences within the boundaries of your faith.

Considerations for religious ceremonies include:

- **Aligning on Rituals and Traditions:** If you and your partner come from different religious backgrounds, choose an officiant who respects and can incorporate aspects from both traditions. Some officiants are skilled at performing interfaith ceremonies, while others may have restrictions.

- **Understanding Religious Expectations:** Some religions have strict guidelines on ceremony structure, attire, vows, or location.

- **Meeting with potential officiants** and discussing these aspects in advance ensures alignment.

- **Location Flexibility:** Not all religious officiants will perform ceremonies outside a specific place of worship, so check if they are comfortable officiating at your chosen venue.

If You're Having a Non-Traditional Ceremony...

Non-traditional ceremonies offer incredible flexibility, from writing custom vows to incorporating unique rituals that reflect your personality.

An officiant could be a non-religious professional or a friend or family member legally ordained online for these celebrations.

Considerations for non-traditional ceremonies include:

- **Creative Freedom:** A professional non-religious officiant often has experience crafting ceremonies that reflect the couple's interests and values. Ask if they are open to incorporating specific rituals, themes, or readings.

- **Tone and Style:** Non-traditional ceremonies can be playful, intimate, or unconventional. An officiant who appreciates your vision and contributes positively to it will elevate the experience.

- **Legality:** Non-traditional ceremonies can sometimes blur the lines of what's legally binding. Ensure your officiant knows local marriage laws and will handle the necessary paperwork, including notarizing the certificate, if necessary.

* * *

Find Someone Who Aligns with Your Ceremony Style

The right officiant should complement the vibe you want for your ceremony. Consider how you want your ceremony to feel and choose someone whose personality and style fit that vision.

1. **Romantic and Sentimental:** If you envision an intimate and heartfelt ceremony, seek an officiant known for their emotional touch and sensitivity.

2. **Lighthearted and Fun:** Some couples want a laid-back or humorous ceremony. An officiant with a witty sense of humor can make guests laugh, cry, and leave with warm memories.

3. **Elegant and Formal:** For a classic, sophisticated feel, look for an officiant who maintains a polished demeanor and understands how to structure a traditional ceremony with a refined approach.

4. **Customized and Personalized:** For those who wish to have a highly personalized experience, an officiant who's flexible and open to incorporating unique elements (like cultural traditions, poetry readings, or meaningful objects) can make a difference.

Make Sure They Understand the Role

An officiant's role extends beyond reading a script. They're the anchor of the ceremony, guiding you through the most important promises of your life. They must understand both the emotional weight and logistical requirements of the role.

- **Pre-Wedding Preparations:** A good officiant will meet with you beforehand to understand your story, offer guidance on the flow of the ceremony, and help craft meaningful vows if needed.

- **Command of the Ceremony Space:** Leading a ceremony means handling the room's attention. A skilled officiant will be comfortable speaking, setting a tone, and creating a natural flow.

- **Legal Responsibilities:** In addition to the emotional and social responsibilities, officiants must complete and submit the marriage license paperwork. Confirm that they understand these requirements to ensure a seamless process.

Questions to Ask Potential Wedding Officiants

Choosing your officiant isn't just about a shared vision but building trust. Here are some essential questions to ask to determine if an officiant is the right fit:

1. **What's your experience with ceremonies like ours?** Their experience with specific ceremony types can reveal whether they're a good match.

2. **Do you have a standard ceremony template, or will you personalize it for us?** Personalization adds warmth and connection to the ceremony, so confirm that they'll adapt it to your love story.

3. **What's your process for preparing for the ceremony?** This can help you understand how much involvement they'll require from you and what to expect in the lead-up to your wedding day.

4. **How do you handle unexpected situations?** From weather changes to tech issues, an experienced officiant will have contingency plans for any situation.

5. **Do you have references or testimonials from other couples?** Reviews can offer insight into how previous couples felt about the officiant's performance and personality.

Final Thoughts

Selecting the right wedding officiant is an investment in the emotional richness of your ceremony. By choosing someone who aligns with your values, ceremony style, and logistical needs, you're ensuring that the heart of your wedding day feels true to your unique love story. With an officiant who shares your vision and brings professionalism and warmth, your ceremony will be one of the most cherished parts of your wedding day.

Beverly Little, CEO/Owner of Tying Knots & Stamping Papers in Alabama

JOIN THE MOVEMENT!
#BAUW

Becoming An Unstoppable Woman With She Rises Studios

She Rises Studios was founded by Hanna Olivas and Adriana Luna Carlos, the mother-daughter duo, in mid-2020 as they saw a need to help empower women worldwide. They are the podcast hosts of the *She Rises Studios Podcast* and Amazon best-selling authors and motivational speakers who travel the world. Hanna and Adriana are the movement creators of #BAUW - Becoming An Unstoppable Woman: The movement has been created to universally impact women of all ages, at whatever stage of life, to overcome insecurities, and adversities, and develop an unstoppable mindset. She Rises Studios educates, celebrates, and empowers women globally.

Looking to Join Us in our Next Anthology or Publish YOUR Own?

She Rises Studios Publishing offers full-service publishing, marketing, book tour, and campaign services. For more information, contact info@sherisesstudios.com

We are always looking for women who want to share their stories and expertise and feature their businesses on our podcasts, in our books, and in our magazines.

SEE WHAT WE DO

OUR PODCAST   **OUR BOOKS**   **OUR SERVICES**

The Ultimate Wedding Guide | 105

Be featured in the Becoming An Unstoppable Woman magazine, published in 13 countries and sold in all major retailers. Get the visibility you need to LEVEL UP in your business!

Have your own TV show streamed across major platforms like Roku TV, Amazon Fire Stick, Apple TV and more!

Learn to leverage your expertise. Build your online presence and grow your audience with FENIX TV.

https://fenixtv.sherisesstudios.com/

106 | Expert Tips and Secrets for Your Dream Wedding

Visit www.SheRisesStudios.com to see how YOU can join the #BAUW movement and help your community to achieve the UNSTOPPABLE mindset.

Have you checked out the *She Rises Studios Podcast?*

Find us on all MAJOR platforms: Spotify, IHeartRadio, Apple Podcasts, Google Podcasts, etc.

Looking to become a sponsor or build a partnership?

Email us at info@sherisesstudios.com

Made in the USA
Columbia, SC
29 May 2025